M000238191

# CREATE IN A *FLASH*

## A LEADER'S RECIPE FOR BREAKTHROUGH INNOVATION

ROGER L. FIRESTIEN, PH.D.

GREEN
TRACTOR
PUBLISHING

P.O. Box 615, Williamsville, NY 14231-0615
greentractorpublishing.com | 716-631-3564
flash@greentractorpublishing.com

ISBN 978-0-692-03627-3 Subjects: Innovation, Creativity, Leadership

Library of Congress Control Number: 2019915643



Art Direction: Cassandra Ott
Editorial: Heather Lazickas
Videography: Dan Richardson
Video Infographic Design: Cher Ravenell

# HOW TO USE THIS BOOK

**Read it. See it in action. Get some tools.**

Welcome to *Create in a Flash: A Leader's Recipe for Breakthrough Innovation*. Read cover-to-cover to experience the Creative Problem-Solving (CPS) process from beginning to end, or drop in to a chapter or story to deep dive on a specific topic. Along the way, you'll find short inspirational stories and access to online resources to help you to put CPS in action.

This icon represents short online videos of Creative Problem-Solving in action. Your creativity cooking lessons! You will also find interviews with innovative leaders who are applying creativity in their organizations to create breakthroughs.
Visit **createinaflashbook.com** to find them all.

At the beginning of each chapter you will also find a list of (free!) downloadable worksheets and templates to use when training your team, teaching about Creative Problem-Solving, or using CPS in your work. Watch for the worksheet icons and access all of them at createinaflashbook.com.

*For Your Innovation* pages are short stories designed to spark personal and organizational creativity.
Get a concentrated jolt of inspiration to help you to see your challenges through a different lens.

Creativity is
the spark
that ignites
innovation.
There is no
innovation
without
creativity.

# TABLE OF CONTENTS

For a community to grow, creative thinking has to happen. We need new ideas. They have to come from somewhere, why not come from us?

Innovation in Economic Developmen
with Jane Fischer

*Chairman, Northern Chautauqua Economic Development Foundation*

# Is this book for you?

*Create in a Flash: A Leader's Recipe for Breakthrough Innovation* is for leaders who realize that in order to grow their businesses, communities, farms, hospitals, schools, universities, associations, churches, synagogues or mosques - the people in their organizations must be able to *create ideas on demand*, instead of waiting for innovative ideas to happen.

Innovative thinking is not something that can be mandated or delegated, so leaders must first develop their *own* creative ability *before* leading their organizations to create breakthroughs.

This book will show you how to be deliberately creative personally, and then how to lead a team to produce innovative results.

In the following pages, you'll learn about the Creative Problem-Solving (CPS) process. It has been used to invent new products, save millions of dollars, effect social change and even save lives. A colleague of mine is using CPS to lead social and educational reform in Myanmar and Colombia. One of my students is using CPS to enact legislation in New York to help curb domestic violence. Dr. Sid Parnes, my CPS mentor, was instrumental in using the process to end apartheid in South Africa.

**Big problems. Amazing solutions. The Creative Problem-Solving process can handle it.**

# 40 years in creativity: Roger's story.

I fell in love with creativity in 1977.

I started college in 1974 as a music major at the University of Northern Colorado. I was teaching guitar lessons to pay for college. I noticed that my guitar students were getting bored with their lessons, and I thought that maybe if I could get my students to get creative with their music, they would enjoy their lessons.

I began reading about creativity and I discovered that there was one place and two names that came up constantly in the literature. Those names were Sid Parnes and Ruth Noller, and the place was the Interdisciplinary Center for Creative Studies at the State University College at Buffalo, NY.

In April of 1977, I was living at home on our farm in Colorado. I got up the courage to call the center from the wall phone in the basement of our house. I talked to the receptionist, Jenney, and I told her about my interest in creativity. She said, "Oh, Dr. Parnes is here. Would you like to talk to him?"

I had never talked to an author before in my life. All of the authors that I knew of were dead. And now, I was going to talk to the creativity rock star, Sid Parnes.

I had a wonderful conversation with Dr. Parnes. He told me about this thing called the Creative Problem Solving Institute — CPSI — and a brand new Master of Science degree in Creative Studies.

When I got off the phone, I was so excited, I was shaking. I bolted up the stairs and told my mom that I had talked to Sid Parnes in Buffalo, New York. Do you know what she said? "*You made a long-distance call?!*" Long distance calls from rural Colorado were expensive in 1977.

In June of 1977 I attended the 24th Annual Creative Problem Solving Institute conference and I took a three-week graduate course. When I returned to Colorado, I was on fire. I knew what I wanted to do with my life.

That fall, I graduated from University of Northern Colorado and was accepted into the master's program at SUNY Buffalo State in January of 1978. Later, I found out that Dr. Parnes was skeptical of me because I was so young.

In June of 1978, I packed up my Ford Maverick and drove across the country by myself. I was 22 years old.

I remember talking to my Mom about coming to Buffalo and studying creativity. I told her, "I don't know if I am going to make any money doing this, but I sure do love it."

I graduated in 1979, and I believe I was just the seventh person to receive the degree. I have never stopped loving this work.

That is not to say that my life and career have had a perfect trajectory. However, it was during those times when I was in my very lowest places that I found by using some of the principles espoused in this book, I was able to survive. And make it through some pretty trying experiences.

When Dr. Parnes retired in 1984, I was fortunate to become a member of the faculty at the International Center for Studies in Creativity at SUNY Buffalo State, and achieved the rank of associate professor. In 1994, I went to a part-time position so that I could run my creativity consulting firm.

As I write these words, I am in my early 60s. Being in this field my entire professional life, I've picked up some bits of wisdom. I would like to share those with you now....

# WHY CREATE

## Why we need to create in a flash.

Most people believe that they are not creative.
Or that creativity is only associated with artists and musicians.
"I can't draw. Therefore, I am not creative." This is a major misconception about creativity - and absolutely false.
Creative thinking (and we all do it!) is what makes us human.

## In this chapter, we'll identify:

- Misconceptions around creativity and innovation
- How we are all creative
- How leaders impact the culture of innovation in their organizations

# Where does all of this start? It starts with you, the leader.

Throughout history, creative, "outside the box" thinking has driven innovation. Johannes Gutenberg, inventor of the printing press, didn't recruit more monks to transcribe books. Henry Ford didn't make a faster horse. Steve Jobs didn't invent a better typewriter. And Airbnb did not build a single hotel.

These folks looked at the world and saw possibilities where others saw the status quo. They used their innate creative ability to invent a better solution... and then proceeded to put it into action.

Today, we're all connected. Life and work are faster and more complex. Our world is smaller, but our problems are bigger.

We desperately need creativity for our survival, but according to research, for the last 30 years our ability to think creatively has declined. Putting Creative Problem-Solving to work for your team will change the game. And we'll start right here.

# Creativity gets a bad name.

I travel on airplanes a lot. You know the airplane routine.

You settle into your seat. The plane takes off and the person next to you strikes up a conversation. For me it goes like this.

> Passenger in seat 4A: "So, what do you do?"
>
> Me in 4C: "I'm a creativity consultant."
>
> 4A: The person usually frowns.
> "A creativity consultant, really? Oh, I'm not creative.
> So, you must be an artist. Do you teach basket weaving?"
>
> Me in 4C: Arugh....

Same scene. Different trip. Different answer from me.

> Passenger in 4A: "So, what do you do?"
>
> Me in 4C: "I'm an innovation consultant."
>
> I watch 4A sit up a little straighter in his seat.
>
> "Innovation consultant! Innovation is very important.
> Our business has innovation in our core values.
> Innovation is in our vision statement. We love innovation."

It never fails. People value innovation, but they're not so sure about this creativity stuff.

But here's the thing. That's like saying,"I want to bake a cake but I'm not so sure about this flour stuff."

**There is no innovation without creativity.**

Creativity is the *spark* that ignites innovation.

# So, what is creativity anyway?

Creativity is complex and there are many definitions of it.

For the purpose of this book, we will use a definition of creativity based on one by Dr. Morris I. Stein.

Creativity: The production of something that is novel **and** useful.

That's it. It's that simple.

If that definition doesn't do it for you. Then try these on for size.

Creativity is a student connecting what matters in his life to a career he can pursue with passion.

Creativity is making an already-tight budget go even further.

Creativity is finding a better way to feed the homeless people in your city.

Creativity is preparing a delicious meal from leftovers in the refrigerator.

Creativity is making bedtime fun to get kiddos to sleep.

Creativity is finding a new way to tell someone that you love them.

Have you done any of those things? Of course, you have. That's what creativity really is.

# The 4-C Model of Creativity:

## Big-C, little-c, mini-c and Pro-c

### We are all creative. Can you find yourself?

### Big-C

Big-C creators are people like **Albert Einstein, Marie Curie, Wolfgang Amadeus Mozart, Sigmund Freud, Charles Darwin, Grace Hopper and Helen Keller.** They are the Nobel Prize winners and the Pulitzer Prize winners. These are the **clear-cut, eminent creative contributors.** Often, their brilliance is recognized after they have passed away.

### little-c

This is **the kind of creativity that we do every day. It is characterized by an unconventional nature, inquisitiveness, imagination and freedom.** little-c creativity is finding a way to fix machinery on the farm with just wire and duct tape, creating a delicious meal using only the leftovers in the refrigerator, or making a quilt using old clothing scraps.

### mini-c

This is the creativity that is part of the learning process and also the creativity seen in young children. As students make personal connections to things they are learning, their insights are considered mini-c.

mini-c is not just for children. It is the "beginner's mind." mini-c **focuses on the creative process.** It is the new idea generated in a brainstorming session that might eventually develop into a breakthrough.

### Pro-c

Pro-c is the creativity of individuals who are **professional creators but have not reached eminent status.** Pro-c is the professional chef who makes a living developing entrees, the musician who composes or writes new musical arrangements, the art director who illustrates books like this, the interior designer who makes your house beautiful, the college professor who creates lesson plans to make a dynamic class experience.

*Anyone who has professional-level expertise in any creative area is likely to have attained Pro-c status.*

# Never, ever say that you are NOT creative again.

If you look at the 4-C model, there is not a single person on this planet who doesn't exhibit some form of creativity. In fact, creativity is crucial to our survival. Imperative to create a dynamic, thriving human experience. **Creativity is in all of us**. You were born into this world with everything you needed to create. You are wired to be creative. You can't help it. It is part of what makes you human.

**Stress is a perceived *lack* of options.**
***Creativity* gives you options.**

# Want to create an innovative organization? Leaders, it's up to you.

Swedish researcher Dr. Goran Ekvall studied the effects of leadership style on the climate for creativity in organizations.

He found that of all of the factors (work load, schedules, marketing activities, meetings, reward systems) that contribute to a company's internal makeup, the leader's behavior alone amounts to 67% of the influence in determining if the organization will be creative.

In other words, if you are the leader and the people in your organization are:

- invested in their work
- contributing ideas
- successfully moving projects forward

...then as far as establishing a climate for creativity in your company, **there is at least a 67% chance that you are doing things right.** If, however, the people in your organization are:

- not involved in the life of the organization
- disinterested or unmotivated in their jobs
- likely to think the organization is a wretched place to work

**...there is a 67% chance that it is YOUR FAULT.**

## So, what are you going to do?

# Leaders: Beware if the water is calm.

## *You* may be toxic.

Imagine the organization you lead is a blue mountain lake.
Look out over the water. What are you seeing?
Is the surface of the lake as smooth as polished glass?
Or are there bubbles in the lake, some waves kicking up,
a little churning here and there?
If there is action in your lake, that's good.
If it's smooth, there is a chance that your lake is stagnant.
Or worse, toxic.

**And who made the lake toxic, you ask?** You did.

| TOXIC LEADER | vs | HEALTHY LEADER |
|---|---|---|
| Aloof | | Approachable |
| Takes credit | | Gives credit |
| Tells | | Listens, seeks ideas |
| Avoids debates | | Explores dissent and differing views |
| Intimidates | | Encourages |
| Rules with fear | | Leads with fairness |
| Blames others | | Takes responsibility |
| Cunning | | Truthful |
| Manipulative | | Allows freedom of expression |
| No direction | | Has Vision |
| Avoids change | | Open to new approaches |
| Moody | | Steady |
| Unaccountable | | Transparent |
| Excludes team from process | | Includes team in process |
| Judgmental | | Accepting and inclusive |
| Self-centered | | Selfless |
| Creates tension | | Fosters a supportive environment |
| Apathetic | | Empathetic |
| Plays favorites | | Supports team members equally |

A toxic work environment leads to stagnation and apathy.

So, cultivate healthy waters! **Positive, forward-thinking leadership will keep the current of growth flowing in your organization.**

# CREATIVITY BASICS

To create in a flash, here is what you need to know.

What if you could LEARN to be creative? Just like you learned to ride a bicycle or drive a car. Most people don't believe that is possible. There is actually a tested recipe for becoming more creative. It is called the Creative Problem-Solving process - CPS.

## In this chapter, we will:

- Learn three types of thinking that are essential for innovation
- Review the research that shows CPS actually works
- Overview the CPS process

  **Online Resources**

Intro to Creative Problem-Solving Video 1
Creative Problem-Solving Model PDF

createinaflashbook.com

I always thought that creativity was something that you had to be born with. I did not realize it was a skill that you could actually build and become better at with practice.

Innovation in Education with Mary Bennett

*Education Coordinator, The Summit Center, Amherst, NY*

Too often we wait for a problem to hit and only then do we try to solve it — at the same time trying to work out the process for doing so. As you have probably experienced, this approach is ineffective, time consuming, and usually results in poor, half-baked solutions.

What would happen if your house was on fire, and the fire department that arrived to save it had to figure out who was going to do what and how they were going to do it? Would you like to be their test case? Neither would I.

Now, just imagine what would happen if the next time a problem confronted your business, you knew exactly ***how*** to go about solving that problem. And further imagine that you trusted the process because you had practiced it and used it successfully.

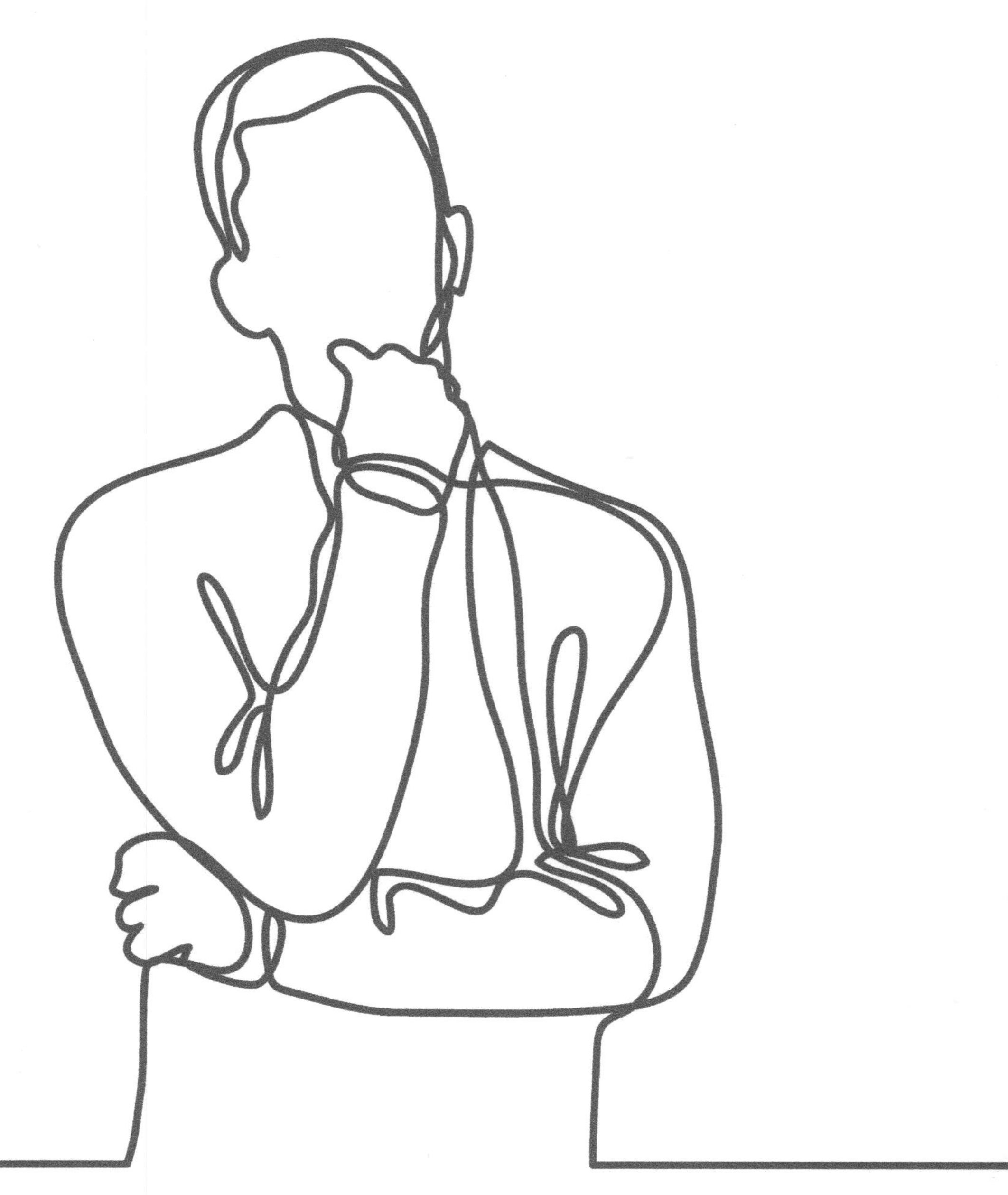

# In order to be deliberately creative, you need to think in three ways.

## Divergent thinking.

Exploring lots of possibilities. Generating ideas that are novel, new, ridiculous, foolish-sounding, weird, goofy, exciting.

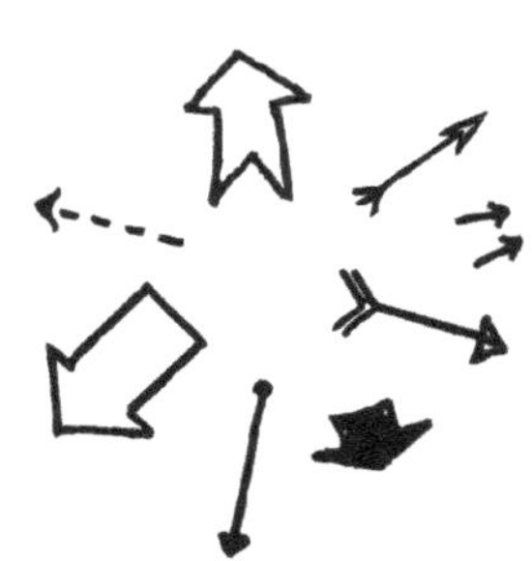

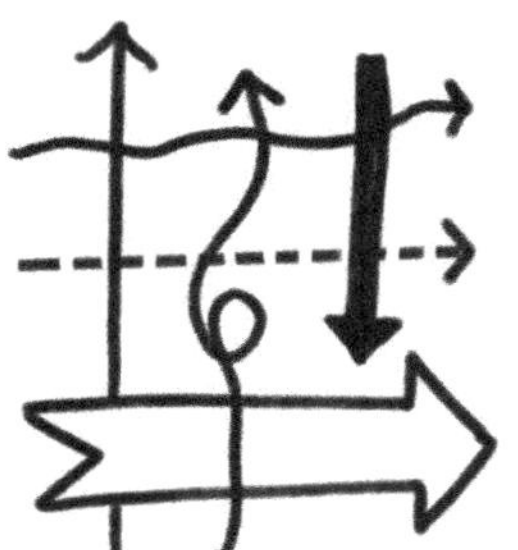

## Combinent thinking.

Combine ideas across areas of knowledge. Connect ideas that seem to be unrelated to the problem you are working on to generate novel ideas.

## Convergent thinking.

Most of us are pretty good at this. Select ideas, sort ideas, test and refine ideas. Make those ridiculous, foolish-sounding, exciting ideas USEFUL.

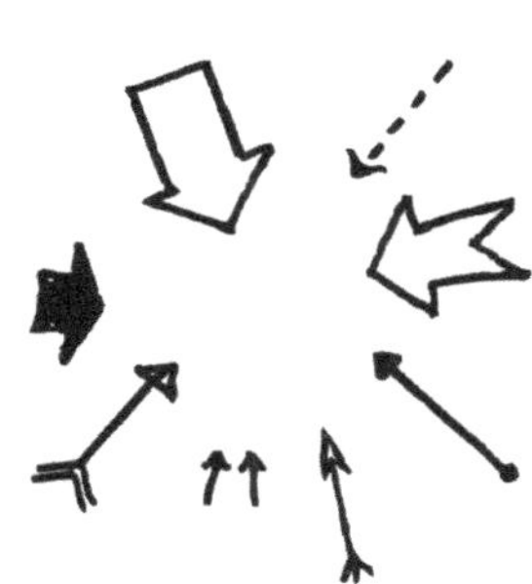

So first, diverge. Next, combine. Then, converge.
How do we know that this works? My research study.

# Creative Problem-Solving works.
## Here's proof.

In my doctoral research I compared creative productivity using CPS-trained groups and ones that were not trained in CPS.

In the study, we used 20 groups of students of five members each who had about 12 hours of CPS training. I compared them with 20 other five-member groups who were not trained in Creative Problem-Solving.

We gave the students a business problem to solve and video recorded the process. We found that the groups that were trained in Creative Problem-Solving showed a significantly higher level of participation. They criticized ideas significantly less and supported ideas significantly more. They also laughed significantly more.

**Did they generate more ideas? Yes! More than 2:1.**

**Effects of CPS Training on Group Communication Behaviors**

| | Untrained | Trained |
|---|---|---|
| Total Responses | 26.0 | 39.0 |
| Verbal Criticism | 2.2 | 0.09 |
| Verbal Support | 1.4 | 3.7 |
| Laughter | 2.1 | 6.0 |
| Smiles | 2.6 | 6.7 |
| Ideas Generated | 13.0 | 27.0 |

**So, how about the quality of the ideas?**

**Idea Quality Results**

| Rated | Untrained | Trained |
|---|---|---|
| 5 | 281 | 618 |
| 4 | 500 | 1,342 |
| 3 | 532 | 917 |
| 2 | 253 | 648 |
| 1 | 29 | 140 |

The groups that were trained in Creative Problem-Solving out-produced the groups that were not trained in Creative Problem-Solving on high-quality ideas by over 2:1 - 618 excellent ideas to 281 excellent ideas. They did great divergent thinking.

A brainstorming session at BBDO advertising agency's New York office in the1950s.

**Bottom Line** The trained groups had a significantly greater chance of a breakthrough occurring simply because there were more high-quality ideas generated than in the untrained group. There were more ideas, and better ideas to choose from.

As a bonus, members of the groups trained in Creative Problem-Solving had a lot more fun generating those ideas than students in the untrained groups.

# Creative Problem-Solving (CPS)

Now you know you are creative. And you know how important the leader's role is in creating an innovative organization. So, how can you make creativity happen — deliberately?

Enter, Creative Problem-Solving (CPS). A simple, repeatable way to take on new challenges and develop innovation solutions that create productive change. CPS is a recipe for deliberate creativity. So, what does the recipe look like?

## STEP 1: CLARIFY THE PROBLEM

First, identify a goal or a wish or a challenge. Then, compile all you know about your goal/wish/challenge to look at the whole picture.

**Diverge:** Generate many ways to redefine the problem
**Tools:** Creative questions
**Converge:** Choose the best problem to solve

## STEP 2: GENERATE IDEAS

**Diverge:** Generate many ideas for solving the problem selected
**Tools:** Brainstorming, brainwriting, Forced Connections
**Converge:** Choose the best ideas to refine and develop

## STEP 3: DEVELOP SOLUTIONS

Ideas have become possible solutions. They are evaluated for their strengths, potential implications and weaknesses (concerns).
This stage of the process polishes out the rough spots in your idea.

**Diverge:** After concerns are identified, generate many ways to overcome them to make the solution stronger
**Tools:** Pluses, Potentials, Concerns and Overcome concerns (PPCo)
**Converge:** Select the best ways to refine the solution

## STEP 4: PLAN FOR ACTION

**Diverge:** Generate all the potential actions you might take to put your solution into action
**Tools:** Planning for action questions
**Converge:** Choose the best actions to take to implement your solution

The beautiful thing about this process is that you won't have to worry about getting creative ideas — they're a natural product of Creative Problem-Solving. And in over 40 years in this business, I have not seen it fail.

STEP 1

# CLARIFY THE PROBLEM

You need to solve the *real* problem.

This is the most difficult stage of the creative process for most people, but also the most critical. Getting this part right sets the foundation for success at finding a solution.

## In this chapter, we will:

- Identify a goal, a wish or a challenge on which you could apply CPS
- Discover the role of gathering data in the creative process
- Learn how to formulate creative questions
- Introduce the "Why? What's stopping me?" method to further challenge your approach to your problem

Identify Your Goal/Wish/Challenge Video 2/PDF
Gather Data Video 3/PDF
Clarify the Problem: Creative Questions Video 4/PDF
Clarify the Problem: Why? What's Stopping Me? Video 5/PDF
Selecting the Best Problem Video 6

createinaflashbook.com

Creativity helps you to NOT look at things as problems. Problems aren't problems anymore. They're just difficult situations and you're trying to find a solution.

Innovation in Agriculture
with Phillip Keppler

*Partner, SK Herefords, Medina, NY*

We have been taught that the initial impression/definition/hunch of a problem is the real problem. We have good reason for this — school already sets up the problem for us. 2+2=4. *What is the capital of Poland?* Warsaw.

**In my entire career, there has only been** one **occasion when the original definition of the problem was the actual problem.**
One **out of thousands.**

That's why we challenge our initial impression of what we think is the problem/goal/challenge. Don't confuse these with ideas...
they are different ways to restate the perceived problem.

You will see in this chapter, Creative Problem-Solving (CPS) is **not** just generating ideas. It is also clearly identifying the best problem to solve.

Leaders in organizations often loathe spending time clarifying the problem. They want to leap to generating ideas. Think about this. It does absolutely no good to generate ideas for solving the wrong problem. The problem we see is the problem we solve. Invest the time identifying the true problem.

When I facilitate a full CPS session, half of the time is spent identifying what the real problem is. The remaining time is spent generating ideas, developing those solutions and planning for action.

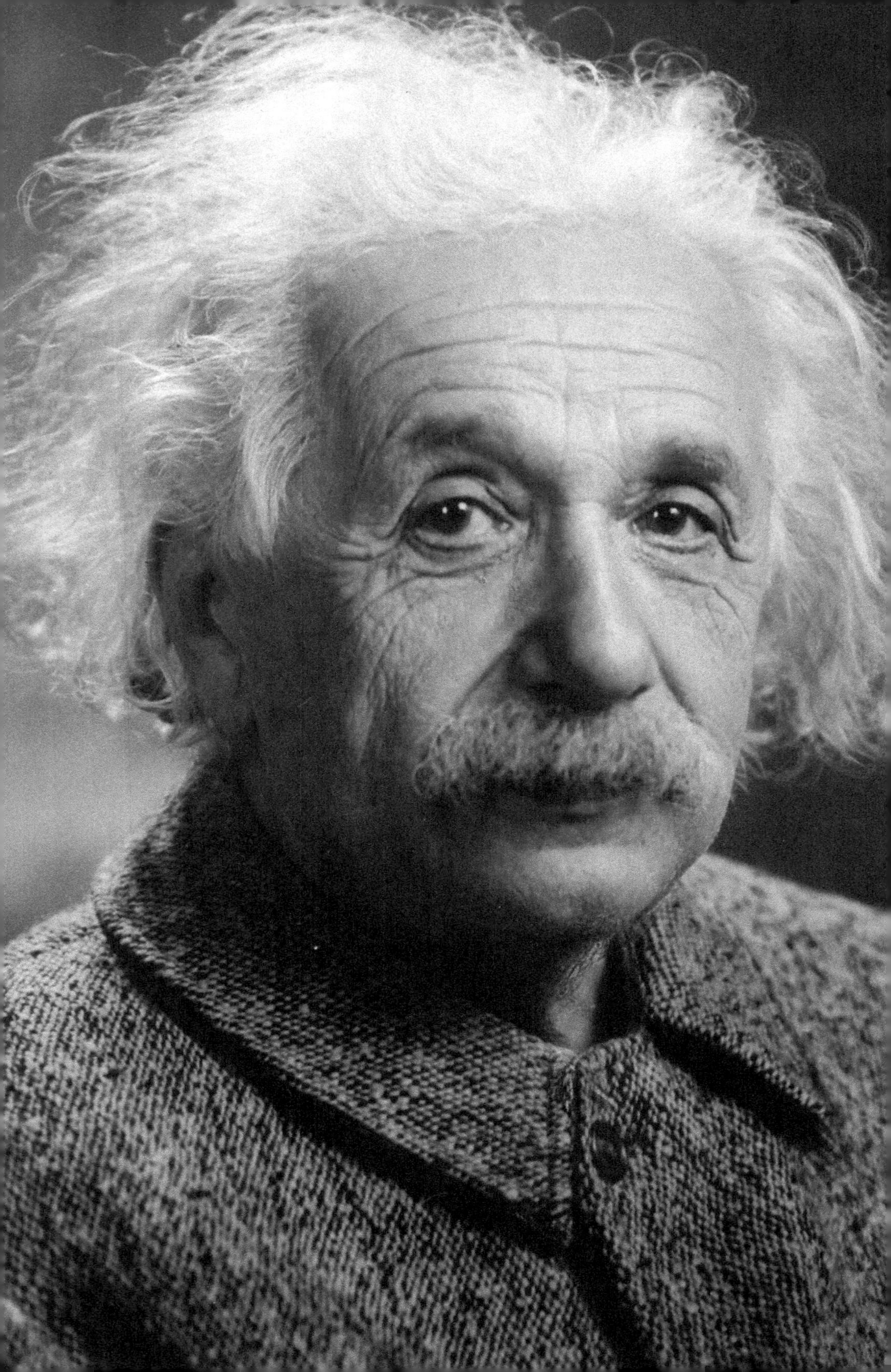

**"The formulation of a problem is often far more essential than its solution."**

Albert Einstein was once asked, "If some imminent disaster threatened the world and you had one hour in which you knew you could save it, how would you spend your time?"

Einstein replied, "I would spend the first 55 minutes identifying the problem and the last five minutes solving it. For the formulation of a problem is often far more essential than its solution, which may be merely a matter of mathematical or experimental skill."

**"It is not enough to just do your best or work hard; you must know what to work on."**

W. Edwards Deming
*Founder of the Total Quality Management movement*

"If you don't wake up in the morning excited to pick up where you left your work yesterday, you haven't found your calling yet."

Mike Wallace

# Identify your goal/wish/challenge.

Creative Problem-Solving. A powerful process. Use it wisely.

If you want to apply CPS, you need to decide what you want to create, invent, solve or improve. I call this identifying your goal, or wish, or challenge.

CPS is a powerful tool. It is designed to help solve those problems or take action on goals that require imaginative thinking and a new perspective. At the beginning of the process, it's common to be unsure of what the real problem is. CPS will help you to discover the real blocks to achieving your goals or visions.

Often when my students begin to apply the CPS process, they sell themselves short. They aim too low. They work on a goal or a wish or a challenge that they think they have the answer to. That is because they have not yet learned to trust the power of the CPS process. Trust the process. Don't waste your time using CPS on simple problems. *What movie to see tonight? Where to go for dinner? How to organize my time better?* You can handle those.

**Creativity is a competitive business weapon.** The organizations that will survive and thrive are not the ones with the deepest pockets. But the ones that can unleash the creativity of their entire workforce.

Use this process to make your life better. To create something great. To do something you're passionate about — something that you believe you could not possibly do. I've consistently seen it work for students and clients, and it's the true power of the process. Creative Problem-Solving can make impossible feats possible.

# Gather data.

We've identified your target, now it's time to gather data. The background information you collect in the gather data step is the foundation for the Clarify the Problem stage. You are creating a clearer picture of the situation that you can carry forward into clarifying the problem.

To gather data, ask questions. Here are five questions that I use consistently to gather data about a goal/wish/challenge.

1. What is the brief history of the situation?
2. Why is this a concern for you?
3. How might this be an opportunity for you?
4. What have you already tried or considered?
5. What might be your ideal outcome for dealing with this situation?

**When gathering data, you are not trying to solve the problem yet.** You are not drawing conclusions. You are collecting what you know and what you feel. You are observing and investigating.

Sometimes just gathering data without judgement can lead to a breakthrough, and the process is done. Problem solved. Goal achieved. Don't skip gathering data, because you could save time and work getting to your desired outcome. Just ask the folks at DuPont.

DuPont makes a countertop product called Corian — you may have some in your kitchen at home. It's known for a stone-like finish and performance, but higher durability and longevity than natural countertop products. Corian is made by robotic machines in a big factory. In one step of production, the proprietary material is rolled through two large drums that press it into the appropriate thickness before being cut to size.

Several years ago, the finished Corian countertop slabs were rolling off the assembly line when operators noticed a BIG PROBLEM. The typically smooth, uniform surface of several pieces in the batch had enormous discolorations. These slabs definitely couldn't be sold. The plant workers poked around looking for the culprit, but couldn't determine the source of the problem. Because it was an isolated issue and the batches had returned to normal, the defects were documented in production logs, and it was back to business as usual.

Over the next few months, the wild blemishes occasionally returned, always sandwiched by long periods of normal production. Finally, the team resolved to track down the source of the issue.

They checked all over the facility, and talked to everyone. And then, someone noticed a drip on the factory floor. Cue the ladders. Before they knew it, someone was up in the rafters discovering — *surprise* — water! The roof was leaking. Drips were hitting the Corian material before it was set, and the ripple was causing the large defects in the finished material.

A look back at the production logs along with historical weather reports showed that each day that the plant experienced damaged batches was also a day when the area saw significant rainstorms. Mystery solved. The roof was patched, the blemishes stopped, end of process. Gathering data is imperative to clarifying a problem, and sometimes it's the solution in itself.

"A problem properly stated is half solved."

John Dewey

# What's keeping you from your goal/wish/challenge?

## Identify the problem that's holding you back.

**How do you identify the real problem? Ask lots of questions.**
Most people associate creative thinking with brainstorming and generating lots and lots of ideas. However, even more important is the stage of the creative process where the real problem is identified.
It doesn't do any good to generate lots of ideas for solving the wrong problem. That's why it's critical to spend time coming up with many different ways to define the problem. Then you can generate solutions for the best definition of the problem.

**For example, you are doing a Google search.**
What is the most important thing to do? Ask a good question.

**You have a tough problem to solve.**
What is the most important thing to do? Ask a creative question.

**When you ask a good question, you get good results. Ask a lousy question you get lousy results. *Ask a creative question, you get creative results.***

When Alex Osborn, the inventor of brainstorming, first coined the phrase **Creative Problem-Solving** in 1953, the idea was unheard of. A problem is no good. Something to be avoided, solved or dispensed of as soon as possible. A problem was certainly something you did not want to play around with, or get creative with. A problem was bad.

## And that's the hook.

A "problem" is not a bad thing. Every problem is just a gap from where you are, to where you want to be.

The revolution in Osborn's approach is that by stating a problem in a creative way, you increase the likelihood of generating creative solutions. Think about it. How can you expect creative ideas if you are not answering a creative question?

**A creative question puts forth what you want to create. Not what you want to avoid.**

To make this very clear: the language you use to describe a problem is going to determine whether you create a good question, a lousy question or a creative question. It also dictates the kinds of solutions you generate.

For example, "We don't have enough money." Good or bad question? Answer: Bad question. In fact, it's a statement.
When you hear that statement, your brain says,
"OK, we don't have any money." Decision made. Move on.

**"How might we raise the money for this project?"**
**"How might we reduce the cost of this project?"**
**Good *and* creative questions.**

Questions framed in this way provoke your mind to search for solutions. They tell your brain. "Let's go find some answers. And because we are using the word 'might,' these can be any answers. We haven't made any decisions yet. Look for options."

Saying, "We don't have enough money," blocks your thinking and sends a message to your brain — "there aren't any ideas out there, don't bother looking."

Give it a try. Next time you need to solve a tough problem, back up a step. Just as you generate creative ideas for solving a problem using brainstorming, you can also brainstorm ways to redefine a problem.

**"But perhaps, the purpose of reframing is not to find the 'real' problem, but to see if there is a better problem to solve."**

**Thomas Wedell-Wedellsborg**

## Use these guidelines to generate creative questions:

1. Defer judgment
2. Strive for quantity
3. Seek wild and unusual questions
4. Combine and build on other questions

Use the phrases below to begin your questions. Then generate lots of questions to get a different view of the problem.

*How might...*

*How to...*

*What might be all the ways to...*

*In what ways might I...*

**When you are redefining the problem, you want questions that open up your thinking.**

Write down at least 15 different ways to restate your problem. Then select the question that describes the main obstacle keeping you from your goal. Only then, begin generating ideas to solve your problem.

Coming up with over 15 ways to restate your problem should only take five to ten minutes. It is time well spent – guaranteed.

**If you want creative ideas, you need *creative questions.* *Lots of them.***

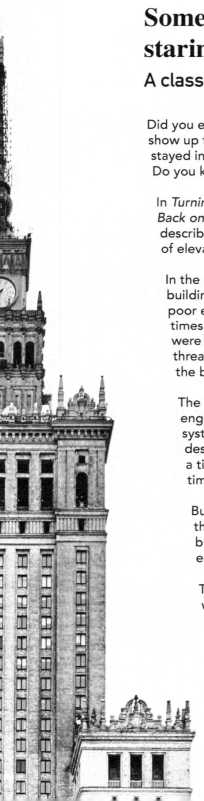

# Sometimes the real solution is staring you right in the face.

## A classic story of redefining the problem.

Did you ever notice that mirrors and elevators usually show up together? I can't think of a hotel that I have stayed in that didn't have a mirror near the elevator. Do you know why?

In *Turning Learning Right Side Up: Putting Education Back on Track*, Russell Ackoff and Daniel Greenberg describe the breakthrough that led to the marriage of elevators and mirrors.

In the mid-20th century in a New York City office building, occupants began complaining about the poor elevator service. According to tenants, waiting times for elevators, especially during peak hours, were excessively long. So long, that several tenants threatened to break their leases and move out of the building.

The manager of the building contacted an engineering firm that specialized in elevator system design and operations. The problem was described to the engineers, who then conducted a time study and determined that indeed, waiting times were excessive.

Building management authorized another study that revealed that because of the age of the building, no engineering solution was economically feasible.

The engineers told management that they would just have to live with the problem permanently.

They were stuck with the elevators they had.

The desperate manager called a staff meeting. Among his staff was a recently-hired graduate of personnel psychology. The manager asked the group to generate possible solutions to the problem. Unfortunately, every idea generated was beaten down by pointing out its faults.

Finally, the room went silent. The only person who had not participated in the botched brainstorming session was the young personnel psychologist.

The general manager singled out the young man and asked him if he had an idea. He told his boss that he was reluctant to express an idea because he saw how the other ideas were rejected when they were presented.

When he did speak, the young man considered the problem not from the mechanical perspective, but from the human perspective. Why, he asked, were riders complaining about waiting for a relatively short time? What if the riders were bored? What if we gave them something to do while waiting?

He defined the problem as, "How might we give riders something to do while they wait?" and, "How might we find something pleasant to occupy riders' time while in the boarding areas?"

His idea: Install mirrors near the elevators so that while riders were waiting they could look at themselves, or surreptitiously check out other riders.

Mirrors were installed.
**Complaints about waiting stopped.**

**A little advice.**
When you are trying to redefine a problem, don't just include the technical experts. Make sure to get an outside perspective, like the psychologist in the elevator story. It is important to involve the people who know what ***can*** be done and to include people who ***don't know what can't be done***. In a good brainstorming session, you'll always get fresh perspectives from people who are not involved with the problem.

# Creative Problem-Solving, man's best friend.

More than 40% of households in the United States have dogs. But the popularity of canine pets has a downside: According to the American Society for the Prevention of Cruelty to Animals (ASPCA), **more than three million dogs enter shelters each year and are put up for adoption.**

Despite heartstring-pulling advertisements showing sad-looking pups, only 1.4 million dogs manage to get adopted each year. That still leaves more than a million *unadopted* dogs, and that doesn't even account for cats and other pets in the same situation.

Enter Lori Weise, the founder of Downtown Dog Rescue in Los Angeles, who challenged the approach that adoption is the only way to define the problem. Weise is one of the pioneers of the shelter intervention program. **Rather than try to get more dogs adopted, Weise reframed the problem as, "How to keep more dogs with their families so that they don't enter shelters in the first place?"**

So, *why* do people give up their dogs? What is the real problem here?

According to Laurie, "Owner surrenders are not a people problem," she says. "By and large, they are a poverty problem. [Many families surrendering their pets]...love their dogs as much as we do, but they are also exceptionally poor. So, when a new landlord suddenly demands a deposit to house the dog, they simply have no way to get the money. In other cases, the dog needs a $10 rabies shot, but the family has no access to a vet, or may be afraid to approach authority. Handing over their pet to a shelter is often the only option they believe they have."

When a family arrives to give up their pet at Downtown Dog Rescue, the staff doesn't just begin the intake process. Instead, they first ask if the family would prefer to keep their companion. If the answer is yes, the staff member tries to help resolve the problem. Today, 75% of pet owners accept help when they learn about the intervention program upon arriving at Downtown Dog Rescue to surrender their pet. **That's 75% fewer animals headed to LA shelters** from Lori's rescue.

There it is. A perfect example of redefining the problem from, **"How to find another home for your dog?" to, "How to keep your dog in your home?"**

**By redefining the problem, Lori and other shelter intervention programs have created a better, a more humane, a more loving solution.**

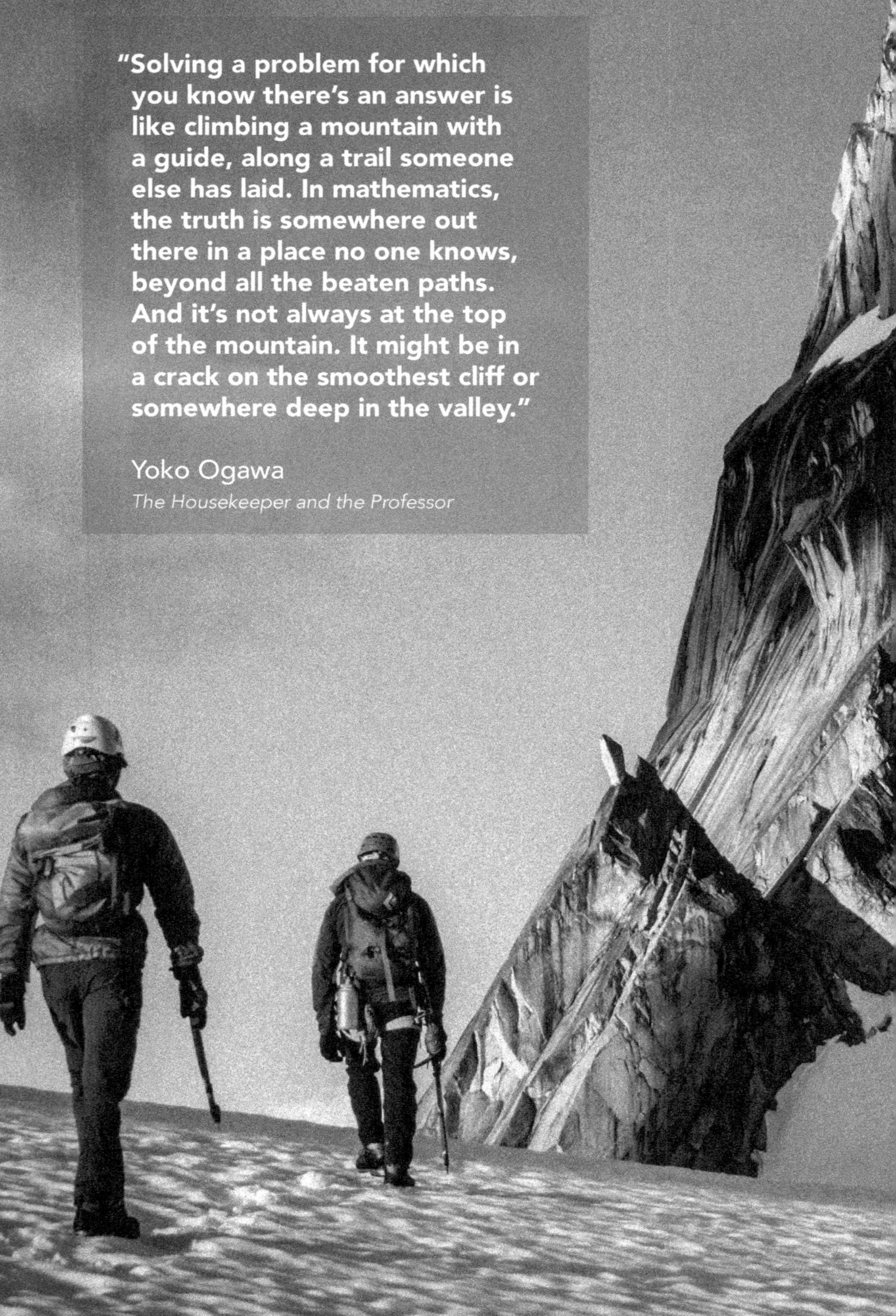

"Solving a problem for which you know there's an answer is like climbing a mountain with a guide, along a trail someone else has laid. In mathematics, the truth is somewhere out there in a place no one knows, beyond all the beaten paths. And it's not always at the top of the mountain. It might be in a crack on the smoothest cliff or somewhere deep in the valley."

Yoko Ogawa

*The Housekeeper and the Professor*

# Ask "Why?"
# Ask "What's stopping me?"

The purpose of generating lots of different ways to define the problem is to challenge the initial definition of the problem. Sometimes it helps to generate lots of creative questions. Sometimes just asking a couple of simple questions will help you to see the problem in a new way.

I recommend asking two questions:
***"Why?" and, "What's stopping me?"***

## Ask *WHY?*

If we go back to our elevator example, the breakthrough solution occurred when the young personnel psychologist asked the question, "Why were riders complaining about waiting for the elevator for a short time?" The problem was not that the elevators were exceedingly slow, the problem was that people were bored.

Lori Weise asked the question, **"Why were people giving up their dogs?"** It wasn't that they didn't love their pets any more, it was because they couldn't afford to care for them. By challenging the problem, Lori gave pet owners alternatives to the single option of giving up their dog.

# "What's stopping me?" in action.

## Dave and Frank's new business.

In the early 1990s my friends Dave and Frank set their sights on creating their very own innovation consulting business. Both of them had various corporate experience, including working in the Frito Lay division of PepsiCo.

Both Dave and Frank were well-trained in Creative Problem-Solving, so they decided to use the "What's stopping me?" question to help figure out what they needed to do to get their company off the ground.

They wrote down their ideal goal on a piece of flipchart paper. Their goal was: It would be great if we had a successful innovation consulting business.

Then they rigorously challenged this goal by asking, "What's stopping us?" The result was a list of everything they needed to do to get the business up and running.

**GOAL** **It would be great if we had a successful innovation consulting business.**

*What's stopping us?*
We don't have a name for the company.

*What else is stopping us?*
We don't have an office to work together.

*What ELSE is stopping us?*
We don't have any brochures.

*What ELSE is stopping us?*
We don't have a plan to get new clients.

*What ELSE is stopping us?*
We don't have a company phone number.

*What ELSE is stopping us?*
We haven't identified our key products.

*What ELSE is stopping us?*
We don't have copy for our marketing.

They did this exercise on a flipchart pad with each barrier listed on a sticky note. As they eliminated each item that was keeping them from reaching their goal, they took the sticky note off the page.

**Eighteen months later, there were no more notes on the page and they celebrated their first million dollars in sales.**

## Now *that's* creating in a flash.

# "What's stopping me?" in action.

## A story about doors.

When you open a door, it swings on a hinge. In buildings like offices, schools or churches, there are two doors at the entrance. One door swings to the left, and the other door swings to the right. Doors keep things in, and doors keep things out.

Now, imagine that it is the early 1950s and you are a delivery truck driver. First thing in the morning, you step up into the cab of your truck.

You drive to the dock, get out, and walk to the back of the truck.

You swing open the left door and then you walk to the right side of the truck. You look around the side of the truck to make sure not to open the right door into the face of a passerby.

You swing open the right door.

You walk back up to the cab of your truck and back it into the loading dock.

You walk to the back of the truck while freight is loaded.

After the freight is loaded, you walk back up to the cab of your truck and get into the cab. You drive the truck away from the loading dock. You stop the truck and get out of the cab and walk to the back of the truck. You swing the left door closed. Then you swing the right door closed. You walk to the front of your truck and get back into the cab.

Now, you begin your route.

Throughout your route, as you drop your deliveries, you follow a similar pattern.

Out of the truck cab. Walk to the back. Swing open the left door. Look around the corner, then swing open the right door. Unload your delivery. Now, because the process takes time, you sometimes leave the truck's back doors open.

If it is raining or snowing, your freight can get wet or damaged. If you have delicious donuts, or cases of fine whiskey in your trailer, there is a chance that while you are inside making your delivery, some nefarious fellow could be helping himself to your load.

If you have a 20-foot trailer and you make 30 stops a day, you will walk more than a half mile a day just to open and close those swinging doors.

So, **what is stopping you** from keeping your freight dry and undamaged? **What is stopping you** from someone pilfering your load while you make deliveries? **What is stopping you** from walking three miles a week to open and close your trailer doors? Could it be the doors?

Time for a story.

Following World War II, Theo C. Whiting, an engineer who helped build the Bell P-39 airplane, left his engineering position with the Bell Aircraft company in Wheatfield, NY. One of his coworkers asked if he knew of anyone who could make garage door panels for his family's garage door dealership. Theo didn't have any contacts, but he told his friend that he would make them himself.

So, Theo starts T. Whiting Engineering and Supply Corporation to build garage door panels in a rented building in Akron, NY. By 1947, T. Whiting Engineering and Supply is manufacturing its own line of Whiting garage doors for residences and commercial buildings.

In the early 1950s, most pick-up and delivery vehicles closed off the back of a truck body or trailer with scissor-gates, vertical tarps, chain curtains or swinging twin panels.

At Stibbs Transportation, a local trucking company, the owner challenged the way the doors worked on his delivery trucks. He began to wonder if a truck could be fitted with a roll-up door like the ones Whiting's employees made for garages. Mr. Stibbs brought the concept of the roll-up truck door to Theo Whiting to see if he could do it.

Theo accepted the challenge. He didn't know how it would be done, but he began to explore how to make the concept a reality while continuing his work on garage doors. Stibbs believed so strongly in the door's potential that he sent 50 of his trailers to Whiting to be fit with roll-up doors.

Then came the fire.

At 3:35 a.m. on December 2, 1953, Mrs. Earl D. Graves of Flint Avenue in Akron was comforting her four-month old daughter when she saw the glow of flames at the Whiting engineering company. Mrs. Graves called in the alarm.

Over 200 volunteer firefighters fought the factory fire, which lit up the sky over large parts of three counties in Western New York.

When the fire was over, the entire plant had burned to the ground, along with five of Stibbs' trailers. All of the inventory, machinery and parts were destroyed, and none of it was insured. The damage was placed at over $200,000, a fortune by 1953 standards.

With no insurance to back him, there was no way Theo could finance the retooling needed to continue making both the garage doors that had been the company's trusted staple, as well as the new, comparatively untested truck doors.

**Instead, Theo Whiting chose to make roll-up truck doors and abandon the garage door business.**

Fast forward to today.

Mike Whiting, Theo's grandson and now executive vice president of Whiting Door Manufacturing, explained that what his grandfather did was a lot more complicated that just sticking a garage door to the back of a delivery truck. "There is a big difference between a truck door and a roll-up garage door. A garage door isn't coming down the highway at 65 miles an hour, hitting potholes and being opened and closed 30 or 40 times a day. On a truck, all of the components have to be stronger to take the abuse encountered on the road and in loading docks."

Today, the truck door market is over $200 million. Whiting remains the leading supplier of roll-up doors in the transportation industry.

**In the case of the roll-up truck door, Theo asking himself the clarifying question - "What's stopping me?" This simple question led to the genesis of a multimillion-dollar business and redefined the way the trucking industry handles freight.**

STEP 2

# GENERATE IDEAS

Generate hundreds of ideas to competition-proof your business and future-proof your life.

The generating of novel, useful, and sometimes impractical ideas. This is what most people associate with creative thinking. Brainstorming is the poster child for Creative Problem-Solving - and you've already been using it! In the previous Clarify the Problem stage you brainstormed ways to nail down your challenge.

## In this chapter, we will:

- Introduce the four rules of idea generation
- Learn how to "warm up" to be creative.
- Review three idea generation techniques:
    - brainstorming
    - Forced Connections
    - brainwriting
- See examples of Forced Connections in action, give pointers to enhance your personal idea-generating skills

  Online Resources

How to do a Warm-up Video 7
Generating Ideas:
Sticky Notes + Forced Connections Video 8/PDF
Generating Ideas: Brainwriting Video 9/PDF
Selecting the Best Ideas Video 10

createinaflashbook.com

I used to come up with a few ideas and chose from those. I realized I needed to be generating more. The deeper we dig, the better the ideas are.

You just have to get the ideas out because you never know. It's natural to want to think '*this might work*,' or '*that might not work*.' One idea might not be the winner, but it might inspire a thought that leads to an idea that leads to an idea that is the winner!

Innovation in Business with Erik Eustice

*CEO/Captain at Of the Sea, a marketing firm in Buffalo, NY*

At this point you've identified the goal, wish or challenge you want to develop a solution for, you've gathered information about what you know about the situation, and you have developed a clearly focused creative question with which you want to generate ideas. Now, it's idea time.

When we use Creative Problem-Solving, generating ideas is where you'll turn the corner from, "Uh-oh, what are we going to do?" to, "Let's come up with lots of ideas for solving this problem." Here's how it breaks down:

First, we warm up. Coming up with good ideas requires an open mind and limber brain muscles.

Brainstorm. There are several tools for generating ideas, but a classic brainstorming session kicks things off. We add different tools and techniques from there.

Then, brainwriting. Forced Connections. Quotas. It's not uncommon to leave a five-minute idea-generating session with 50 or 60 ideas for solving a problem. Really.

You've set the stage for success in the idea-generating stage, now let's go out and get 'em.

# How do you ruin a waffle iron?

## What sneakers and waffles have in common.

One summer Sunday morning in 1971, Bill and Barbara Bowerman were fixing waffles for breakfast. Bill, the head running coach at the University of Oregon, was bemoaning the fact that his runners didn't have track shoes that could grip the new artificial turf.

Having coached 33 Olympians, he was always on the lookout for better athletic gear. In the 1960s he had co-launched a company to import lightweight running shoes from Japan. He even had a lab in his house where he could experiment.

Now he was looking for a lighter, faster shoe, one without spikes that could still grip the new running track.

At that moment, Barbara pulled a waffle off the hot waffle iron. Staring at the waffle, Bill suddenly made a connection. The grid pattern on the waffle might just create the perfect grip for the sole of a running shoe. He grabbed the waffle iron and ran to his lab.

By the end of the day, he had prototyped the shoe that would earn him his first patent and launch his company to international fame: the Nike Waffle Trainer.

**How did it happen? Bill was searching for wild and unusual ideas. His mind was wide open. And when his breakfast landed on the plate, Bill looked beyond his stomach and saw sneakers.**

When his waffle breakthrough came to him, Bill Bowerman had been working on the problem for months. What if we could speed up the creative process? Or, better yet, what if we could make this connection-making process **deliberate**?

Scary thought — what if Barbara had been making *pancakes*?

It's easier to get a creative idea than it is to ride a bicycle.

**Just follow the directions.**

Alex F. Osborn, the inventor of brainstorming

# Directions for riding a bicycle.

1. Grab the handlebars of the bicycle with both hands.
2. Place your right leg over the top of the bicycle.
3. Place your right foot on the pedal on the right side of the bicycle.
4. Make sure the pedal is close to its highest point in the rotation.
5. Straddle the seat on the bicycle while keeping your left foot on the ground for stability.
6. Push up on your left foot while pushing down on the right pedal with your right foot.
7. Sit down on the seat as the bicycle stabilizes in a vertical position.
8. Continue pushing down on the right pedal.
9. As the left pedal rises, push down on the left pedal with your left foot.
10. Continue to hold on to the handle bars.
11. Repeat as you are moving the bicycle forward.

**Do you honestly think you could learn to ride a bicycle by reading those directions?**

**That's what many people think they can do with their team when it comes to being creative. Just read the brainstorming directions - *voila!* All of a sudden, the team produces a torrent of creative ideas.**

# That's just ridiculous.

# Why do people find it easier to ride a bicycle than to be creative?

Because they have ***practiced*** riding a bicycle. They have not ***practiced*** getting creative.

Great sports teams practice. Great symphony orchestras practice. Fire departments practice. They all practice so that when they must perform at peak effectiveness under extremely stressful conditions, they can execute extremely well.

# Directions for idea generation.

1. Defer judgment
2. Strive for quantity
3. Seek wild and unusual ideas
4. Build on other ideas

**Question:** When do we practice team problem solving?

**Answer:** Usually, we don't.

The directions for idea generation are profoundly simple. They are **easy to do**. But they are also just as easy **NOT** to do.

# Practice getting creative by warming up.

Just as athletes need to stretch before a physical workout, participants need to stretch their idea generating muscles before getting to work on the main issue.

**How to warm up:**
Before you do an idea generating warm-up exercise, get a facilitator to manage the process. Review the guidelines for generating ideas:

1. Defer judgment
2. Strive for quantity
3. Seek wild and unusual ideas
4. Build on other ideas

Present the problem to be solved worded as a creative question. Creative questions always begin with the words, *"How to...," "How might...," "In what ways might I...,"* or *"What might be all the...?"*

Then, the group generates ideas following the idea-generating guidelines. As ideas surface, participants voice them to the group. The facilitator records them on a flipchart, or the participants write ideas on sticky notes and hand them off to the facilitator, who places the ideas on the flipchart.

During a warm-up session, give the group a time limit and a quota for the number of ideas generated. I like a quota of 25 ideas and a time limit of five minutes.

Most warm-up exercises are admittedly silly. They're designed that way on purpose. The subjects are common and non-threatening. Many of the ideas suggested will be absurd or impractical. That's exactly the imaginative mindset the group needs when they eventually approach the "serious" problem. Don't let the "silly" factor deter you.

## Why do a warm-up? Three reasons.

First, to briefly train the group in the brainstorming method.

Second, to "sanction" the time for speculation. In this session we are going to think differently than how we have been thinking up to this time. This is the time to look for unusual ideas.

Finally, we do a warm-up exercise to create a judgment-free zone. There's no judging when you are generating ideas.

## When selecting a warm-up:

Make it simple.

Make it *fun*.

**Here are some of my favorite warm-up topics. Pick a few and try them out.**

- What might be all the ways to improve a refrigerator?
- How to get a hippopotamus out of a bathtub?
- What might you do with ten tons of orange Jell-O?
- How to get a bear out of my living room?
- How to get a raccoon out of a mini-van?
- What might you do with 50,000 bowling balls that are flat on one side?

# FYI *For Your Innovation*

## Don't get fat. Get a facilitator.

Last year, I started working with Joe and Brandon, personal trainers at a local fitness facility. I wanted to take off some weight and get rid of some of the aches and pains I was beginning to experience. My goal was not to get ripped abs like I had when I was 30. Ok, I didn't have ripped abs when I was 30. I wanted to slim down and feel better.

Could I have done it without a trainer? Probably, but not likely. I hadn't made much progress on my own so far.

Joe and Brandon do a number of things for me. They show me how to exercise with proper form so that I don't get hurt. They keep me on track so that my needs are met. They make sure that all of the conditions that I need to accomplish my goals are in place. They hold me accountable.

My only job is to focus on doing my exercises correctly, following the fitness plan we have established, and letting the process work. That's it!

**Fitness trainers are like Creative Problem-Solving facilitators**

Health and fitness trainers are a lot like Creative Problem-Solving facilitators. Can you run effective Creative Problem-Solving sessions consistently without someone managing the process and keeping the group on track? My experience is, no.

A facilitator keeps the creative process moving, ensures that the needs of the client and the group are met, and knows the creative process inside and out. Good group facilitators make sure that participants' ideas aren't destroyed, and that the session produces results that work.

A facilitator holds the team accountable to the process so that it can accomplish its goals instead of wasting time spinning its wheels. Just like a good trainer.

Comparing the qualities of fitness trainers and Creative Problem-Solving facilitators, you will see some striking similarities.

| Fitness Trainers | CPS Facilitators |
|---|---|
| Design the exercise program | Design the innovation session |
| Manage the fitness process | Manage the creative process |
| Keep the client on track | Keep the group on track |
| Know the exercises inside & out | Know the process inside & out |
| Are responsible to the client | Are responsible to the client |

If a good trainer can help me accomplish my fitness goals, an excellent facilitator can help you keep ahead of your competition and create breakthroughs that work.

**A decision is the end. An idea is just the beginning.**

# Defer judgment.

Now you're all warmed up. The most important behavior to practice when you are generating ideas is to deliberately separate your imaginative thinking from your judgmental thinking. Don't judge your ideas while you are generating them.

Because an idea is just an idea.
It is not an action.
It is not a decision.
It is not a conclusion.
It's just an idea. That's it.

Write down every idea. Don't try to change it or modify it.
Just write it down.

Judge your ideas *after* you have generated them, not *while* you are generating them.

When most people think about generating ideas they imagine a group furiously writing ideas down on sticky notes and a facilitator sticking those ideas up on a flipchart.

You don't need a group to generate ideas. Just follow the guidelines for generating ideas when you are working alone.
Artists jot down their ideas as sketches in sketchbooks.
Musicians sing melodies and lyrics into their smartphones.
The focus is to gather ideas *without* judging those ideas.

**Generate first. Judge later.
Never do both at the same time.**

# Lessons from photographers:
## Strive for quantity.

I went to a terrific wedding a couple of years ago.

The ceremony was at one of the oldest churches in Buffalo, NY. There were three photographers at the ceremony. The reception was at an old armory turned into a banquet hall. The three photographers were there too. They were constantly taking pictures.

We ate great food and drank wonderful wine. As the evening was winding down, I decided to take a stroll around the armory. I found the three photographers in a side room putting together their end-of-evening show.

> Me: *So how many pictures did you guys take tonight?*
>
> Boss photographer: *We took about three.*
>
> Me: *Three? You guys were all over the place tonight.*
>
> Boss photographer: *We took 3,000 pictures.*
>
> Me: *3,000? Really, 3,000?*
>
> Boss photographer: *Yes, 3,000. We show the bride and groom about 900. They pick about 50. We delete the pictures they don't pick.*

50 pictures are less than 2% of all the pictures taken that day.

**Think of ideas like photographs. They are free, and we always get more than 2% good ideas.**

The ideas you don't use, you can delete.

# Want to get new ideas?

## Set a quota.

How many ideas do you need to get a good one? Do you have to come up with hundreds of ideas to get a breakthrough?

It all depends on the kinds of ideas you want.

If you want to find ways to improve the way you are currently doing your business you will need fewer ideas than if your goal is to completely redefine the nature of your business or your life.

We can't precisely predict the number of ideas you will need to get a new insight, but setting an idea quota helps.

Between 40-50 ideas is a reasonable quota if you want to generate ideas to improve your current practices. More than 50 ideas will help you begin to really stretch your thinking, but if you want to completely redefine the work you are doing and create some disruptive ideas, a quota of 100 ideas or more is not unreasonable.

After analyzing hundreds of idea-generating sessions, there was a trend that emerged. It was the one-third; one-third; one-third principle.

Let's say your goal is to generate 40 ideas for solving a problem. The first 10 to 12 ideas usually don't produce any breakthroughs. These ideas are the ones that people have thought of before. The silly ideas will surface from about idea 12 to 24. Finally, new ideas and insights typically occur after idea 30.

To take this principle a bit further, the first third tend to be the obvious and incremental ideas, the second third are the ridiculous and sometimes brilliant ideas and the last third are the game changers and disruptors.

**So, what is the bottom line? If you are consistently generating 10 to 12 ideas in your idea generating sessions and you think you are getting creative, you're not.**

**The creativity comes in the stretch. The innovation comes in the stretch. Go for the third one-third, you'll be glad you did.**

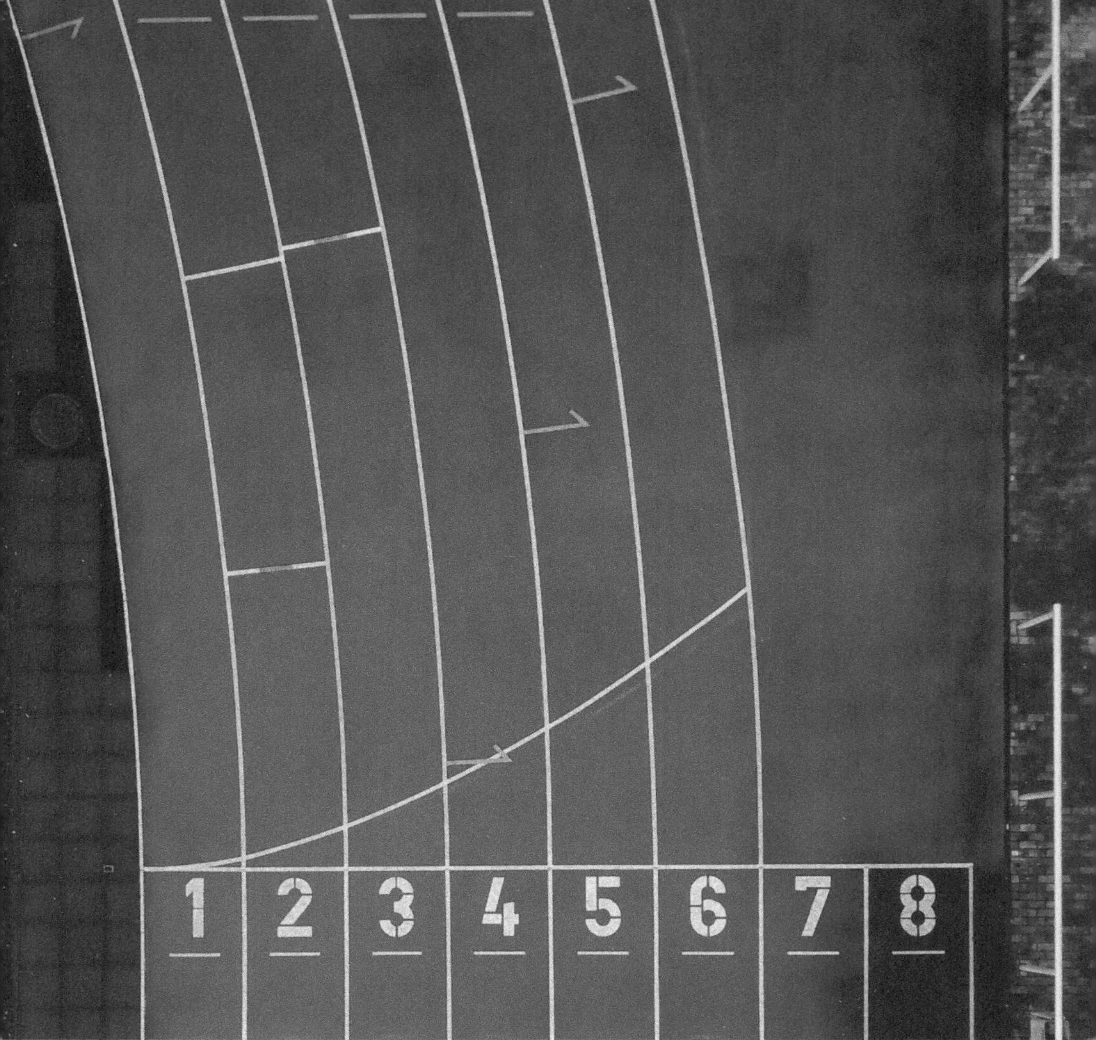


# The law of large numbers

The "quantity breeds quality" principle demonstrates the mathematical theorem, "The law of large numbers." It states that when analyzing "the difference between the number of successes and the number of trials, the expected number of successes tends to grow as the number of trials increases."

The more pictures you take, the greater the chances of capturing that amazing moment.

Ideas are the same. The more ideas you have to choose from, the greater your chances of getting a good one.

# Want to get those numbers up?
## Try brainwriting.

When a group uses brainwriting, the participants don't have to talk to each other because each person writes their ideas on a brainwriting grid.

When conducting a brainwriting session, begin with a stack of blank brainwriting grids. Each square of the grid will contain a blank sticky note. Each participant begins with a blank grid, and several extras are placed in the middle of the table or work area. Here's how it works:

1. Participants write the problem statement/creative question at the top of each grid.
2. Use the guidelines for generating ideas: defer judgment, strive for quantity, seek wild and unusual ideas, and combine and build on other ideas.
3. Participants write three ideas on the first open row of the brainwriting grid. One idea per box.
4. After writing three ideas, participants place the form in the middle of the table and pick up a different grid that another participant has started. If there are none, they start with another blank grid. With extras in the middle, no one has to wait for other members of the group. A grid will always be waiting for them.

Ideas can be new, or they can build on ideas already generated. When brainwriting, participants should take time to read other ideas on the grids as they may inspire new ideas. Participants then repeat the steps, filling the grids. Continue and add more pages as needed. Aim for eight to ten full brainwriting grids. After you fill the grids with ideas, add them to the other ideas you generated using brainstorming.

**It has been my experience that a brainwriting session usually produces about twice as many ideas as traditional brainstorming session. Here's why:**

- People who are reluctant to talk in a brainstorming session can express their ideas.
- Contributions are relatively anonymous.
- The facilitator can sometimes create a bottleneck during a brainstorming session. There's no waiting with brainwriting.

**By using a combination of traditional brainstorming first, and then brainwriting, it is not uncommon to generate 70 ideas in ten minutes (really!) If your group is trained in Creative Problem-Solving, this number jumps significantly.**

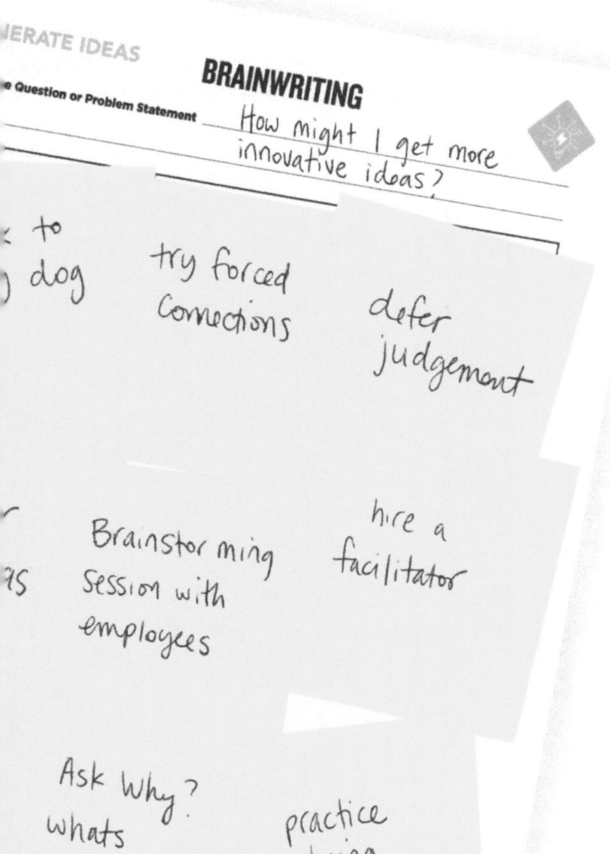
ERATE IDEAS
BRAINWRITING
Question or Problem Statement
How might I get more innovative ideas?
to
dog
try forced connections
defer judgement
Brainstorming session with employees
hire a facilitator
Ask Why? whats stopping me?
practice being creative

**If you follow the guidelines for generating ideas *and* *PRACTICE*, you will create in a flash.**

If you don't, you won't.
It's that simple. **Guaranteed.**

**A word of caution.**

**Do not start off an idea generating session with brainwriting. Always do a brainstorming session first, then add brainwriting.** By doing this, the brainstorming session acts as a warm-up for the group. If a member of the group gets stuck or slows down while they are brainwriting, they can look at the ideas that were generated with brainstorming and build on those ideas.

**"I've learned the importance of connections. Before, I would not think about connecting this idea to another idea, but you've got me thinking that way. Even though two things may seem totally unrelated, you made me think maybe there is a relationship.**

**Creative thinking is connecting ideas in a different way than we have traditionally."**

Dr. Robert Gatewood

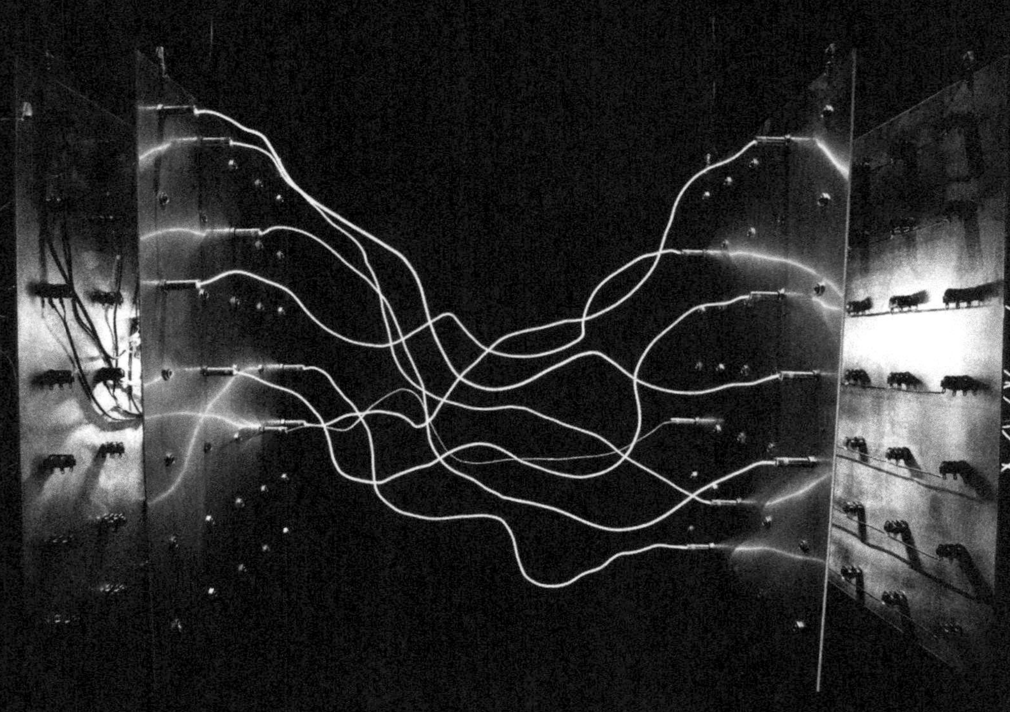

# Force connections to create new ideas.

## Seek wild and unusual ideas.

Most breakthroughs come by connecting things that are not usually considered connected. Often these connections occur as if by chance. You are working on a tough problem, you are stymied for a solution, so you take a step back. Then, you see something unrelated to your problem and you make a connection. Unfortunately, you had to wait to make that connection. What if you could make those connections on demand?

In the world of Creative Problem-Solving, we have a technique for this called Forced Connections. It is my go-to method to help increase combinent thinking.

**Forced Connections is the essence of creativity; the practice of combining ideas that don't appear to be related in a new way. This method helps you get ideas flowing when you're stuck.**

**How it works:**

1. **Consider the problem you are trying to solve.**
2. **Pick an object or situation that is completely unrelated.**
3. **Find or "force" a connection between the problem you are working on and the seemingly unrelated object.**

**The result of this new connection is a** new idea.

Here is an example. Let's say you work for the ACME bathtub company. You have been trained in Creative Problem-Solving methods and your boss has asked you to facilitate a group session to generate some ideas on how to make ACME bathtubs better. Your creative question is:

"What might be all the ways we can improve our bathtubs?"

The group starts generating ideas to improve your bathtubs and after a few minutes they slow down.

They have generated the usual ideas for improving a bathtub. But now they are stuck and their ideas have dried up. It's time to introduce Forced Connections. Pictures work great to stimulate new thinking. So, you whip out a picture. The first picture you show is a bunch of bananas. You ask them:

*"What ideas do you get to improve a bathtub from bananas?"*
The group generates ideas like: make it non-slip, make it yellow, put a soft bottom in the tub, shape the tub to fit your body and — have a bunch of my friends over.

*You show another picture: a photo of a beautiful beach.*
The group generates ideas such as: put salt water in the tub, serve cocktails in the tub, a tub for two, have soothing ocean sounds and an outdoor tub.

*One more picture to complete the exercise: an airplane cockpit.*
This picture generates ideas like: put in temperature controls for the tub, put lots of windows around the tub, put seats in the tub and make the tub fly.

You don't need pictures to have this technique work for you. All you need to do is look around. As I write this, I am sitting at my desk. If I were working on a challenge and got stuck, I would ask myself — what ideas do I get from my telephone, or books on my bookcase, or the fan on my desk, the trees in my backyard or the model rocket that I built when I was 12?

**Using Forced Connections, the ideas you get may not be the breakthrough ideas you are looking for, but the technique gets the idea-generating process moving again so you can dig deeper to get to those breakthroughs.**

Oh, and bathtubs really can fly.

*Johannes and Philip Mickenbecker's bathtub drone.*

# Forced Connections in action.
## Using Whac-A-Mole for social change

Have you ever played the arcade game "Whac-A-Mole?"
Five holes that each contain a single plastic mechanical mole.
One soft black mallet.

When the game starts, the moles begin to pop up from their holes at random. The object of the game is for the player to force the moles back into their hole by bopping them on the head with the mallet. When you whack a mole back into its hole, you get a point. The faster you whack, the higher your score.

Community organizer Dianne Britain was brainstorming at a community meeting in Buffalo, NY about how the citizen group could disrupt a school board meeting in order to get a vocal racist off of the board. The board needed to be unanimous in their vote to remove the racist member, but there were two board members voting to keep him.

The group's objective was to illustrate that they were an organized community and to be disruptive enough that their voices would be heard by the two holdout board members. They needed the board to know that they were not going anywhere until the objectionable member was removed.

In the brainstorming session, Dianne showed the group a picture of an old arcade room. In the room was a Whac-A-Mole game. **The group quickly built on an idea and came up with a plan.**

At the next school board meeting, the group broke into five groups of six people positioned in different parts of the room. As the meeting began, one group stood up and started chanting. When police approached the group, the group sat down and another group on the other side of the room stood up to chant. This bounced from group to group around the room.

The trick? They couldn't be arrested or escorted out of the room while sitting down. This went on for an hour.

**End result: No arrests at the meeting. No one escorted out of the meeting. Eventually, the racist board member was removed. Creative Problem-Solving for the win.**

"The unexpected connection is more powerful than one that is obvious."

**Heraclitus**
*Philosopher, Persian Empire*

# FYI *For Your Innovation*

## Where are your best ideas born?

## The power of incubation.

**I'd bet you a hundred dollars that you don't get your best ideas at work.** Most people in my seminars and classes tell me that they get their best ideas while driving a car, exercising, taking a bath or shower, or as they fall asleep at night.

At work, most of us are in implementation mode. Action mode. Make-it-happen mode. When we get away from work and are able to pay attention to something in a relaxed way, new ideas begin to surface. **Activities like driving, bathing or falling asleep are so automatic that we relax the judgmental part of our thinking, thus allowing new ideas to surface.**

A classic tenet of creative problem solving is that **often breakthrough ideas come to us when we step away from the problem and *incubate*.** You've likely experienced it yourself. You've been working on a problem for a long time, haven't made progress, and you back off to do something else. **After your period of incubation — *eureka!* The idea hits you.**

Several times in my life I've woken up in the middle of the night with a breakthrough idea for a project I am working on. As a matter of fact, my first book came to me at 3 a.m. in Washington D.C. in 1986. I was finishing up my doctoral dissertation and took the weekend off to visit some friends. I still remember the meal we had that evening, Thai food with white wine. In the middle of the night, I woke up with the characters and the plot line for the book. I grabbed my pocket tape recorder and dictated almost the entire book. The next morning, I needed a new tape because I had filled one with my early morning epiphany. Now, here is the kicker. I went to D.C. to get away from my work. I almost did not take the recorder with me because I thought I was mentally exhausted. However, if I had left the recorder behind, I am sure that book would not exist today.

Recently, I had the pleasure of moderating a panel of entrepreneurs for one of my clients. Each member of the panel agreed that their best ideas don't come at work. **All of them had their best ideas "off the grid."** One entrepreneur goes to his cottage on the lake, another goes to his property in the desert, another works on a friend's cattle ranch outside of the city. (Confession: I'm the guy at the ranch. Meet my bovine friends on page 89!) Several of them keep their phones near their beds so they can dictate a voice memo if they wake with an idea during the night.

My friend Michelle Miller-Levitt was on the panel. She owned Buffalo's first podcast studio, *Too Much Neon*. Michelle told me where she goes to find great ideas, and it's one of the most unusual "places" I've ever heard. When Michelle is stuck on a problem, she hangs upside down on a medicine ball. She says that by doing this, she sees the world a little differently. After a few minutes, she has cleared her mind and a new idea usually surfaces.

The key? Being ready to catch those ideas when they appear. Keep a notepad or your smart phone with you to record new insights when you're in the mode.

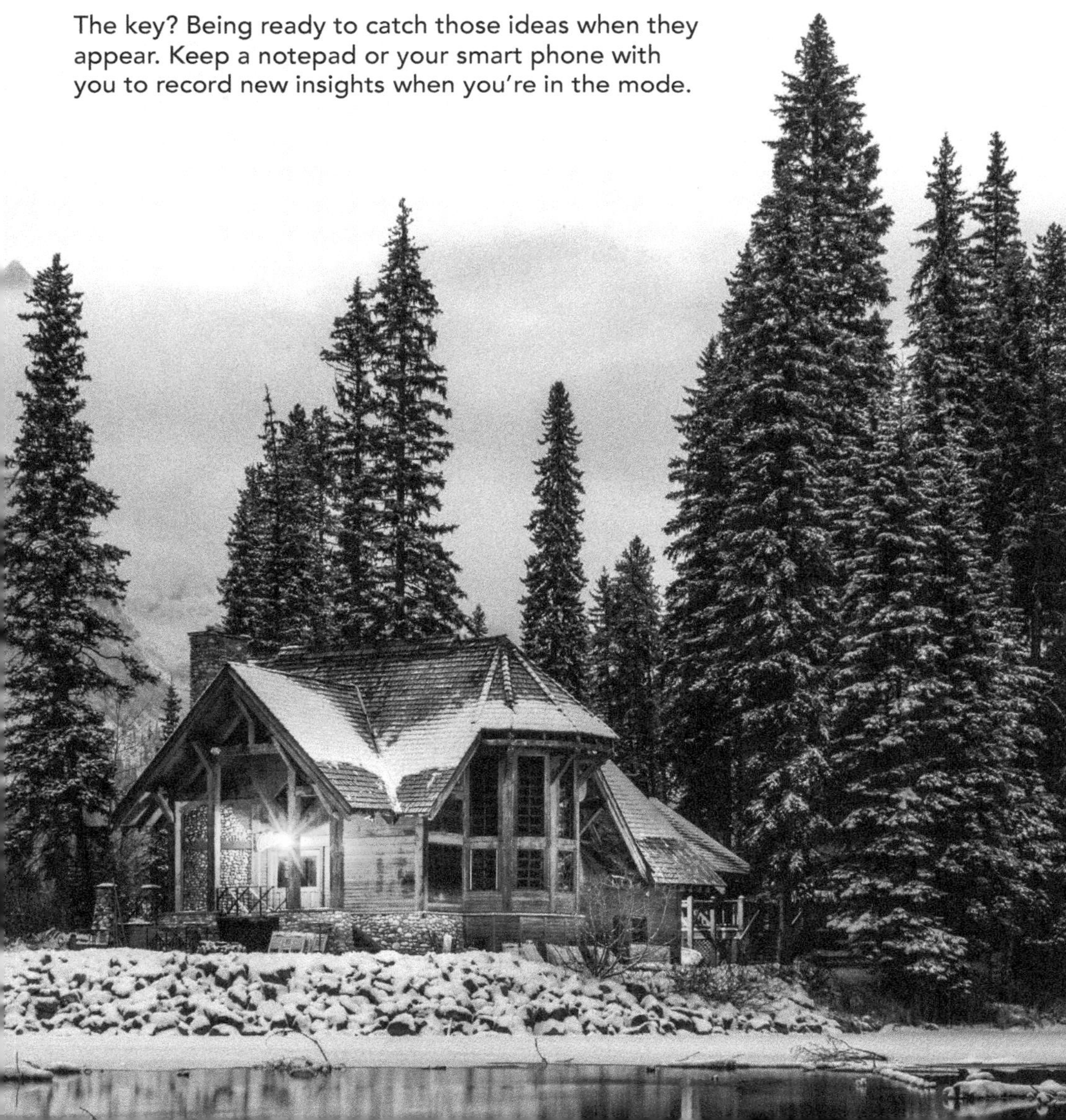

# FYI *For Your Innovation*

## Drive a tractor. Get creative.

Some of my best ideas come to me when I am driving a tractor on the SK Herefords ranch near Medina, NY. The ranch is owned by my friend Phil Keppler and his business partner David Schubel. SK Herefords grazes 400 head of cattle on 800 acres of land, and it's where I go when I need "farm therapy."

For me, farm therapy is spending at least one day working on a farm.

I know when I need farm therapy. My writing starts to get a little stale. I find myself beginning to be frustrated by the everyday things that running a creativity business and teaching at a university entail.

Here is why farm therapy at the SK Herefords ranch works for me.

It is a change of pace. Walking around in muck boots in six inches of soupy cow manure sure is a change of pace from giving a talk in a well-appointed lecture hall.

So is driving a tractor, bush-hogging 30 acres of fields to prepare the land for the cattle to graze. Tractor time gives me time to think.

While I do need to pay attention when I am bush-hogging, it isn't the same as writing a book, teaching a class, or giving a speech. (If you are unfamiliar with a bush-hog, think of a 20 foot-wide lawn mower.)

Farm therapy provides me with a clearly visible measure of accomplishment. I feel a real sense of satisfaction when I look back over an evenly-mowed field that was dotted by clumps of tall weeds and uneven growth just hours earlier.

In my usual work, I don't have the luxury of seeing that immediate and visible accomplishment. Students may begin to think differently after they have been in one of my seminars, but I can't *see* that change.

Finally, when I'm on the farm, the decisions are up to someone else. In my daily life I have to make countless decisions, just like you. When I go to the farm, Phil makes the decisions for me. Phil tells me what to do, and we make it happen.

"Let's move those hay bales off the north 40." We go do it.

"We need to feed cattle at David's place." We load up the feed truck, and off we go.

It's that simple. I don't have to make the decisions. I just go, and I do the job. I'm amazed by how refreshing it is. After farm therapy, I can almost guarantee that I will gain a new insight into a problem I am working on. A great idea crystalizes for a chapter in a book, or a new insight for a program design presents itself.

**To nurture your creativity, find your own form of farm therapy.** Whatever your farm therapy is, make sure that it has these three attributes:

1. It is a change of pace from your usual activities.
2. You can see a tangible result from your actions, so you can feel a sense of accomplishment.
3. You don't have to make decisions as to what to do next.

**That's it. Find an activity that fits those criteria, go out and do it.** You will be amazed at the impact it will have on your clarity and your creative muscles when you break from your routine. Truth be told, I have taken a few falls into soupy cow manure when my muck boots have gotten stuck. Now that's a change of pace!

# FYI *For Your Innovation*

## Don't talk to the same people.

Alan Gozdalski has taken care of the landscaping on my property for over 20 years. He treats my property like his own. When a devastating fall storm hit Buffalo, NY in October of 2006, Al was one of the first people who called me to check on how his (my) yard fared. I am pretty sure that we both had tears in our eyes when we walked the property and found ourselves shoulder-high in a sea of broken trees.

Al is one of the most creative entrepreneurs I know. He pioneered residential ponds in Western New York, and since 1997, he has installed over 1,000 ponds in the area, including one in my yard.

Every year I host a holiday party at my house. I invite clients, friends, students and interesting people who have become friends. Al comes to the party.

I was at Al's store recently, and he introduced me to another customer. He made a point of telling them about my parties.

"I met a plethora of interesting people at Roger's party. In five minutes, I talked to five different people with different ethnic and work backgrounds. I met a nun, a cardiologist, a rock musician who is in the Buffalo music hall of fame, a Pilates instructor, farmers, branding experts, website designers, entrepreneurs, corporate presidents, college professors and some of Roger's graduate students that are different ages and nationalities."

Al loves my party. Why? Because at the party, he is exposed to people who don't think the same way he does.

**One of the most effective ways to get creative is to interact with people from varying backgrounds who have a variety of interests.** This isn't always easy to do, for most of us find it more comfortable to spend time with people familiar to us. To our own detriment, we often don't make the time or effort to meet new people.
I am pretty sure that we violate the fire code by packing so many people into the house at the holiday party. You can't help but meet new people when you come. And, if I know two people who would enjoy talking with one another, I make a point to pull them aside to make an introduction.

Research conducted on communication networks determined that **the best source of new information is NOT from the people you see regularly. Why? Those people usually have the same information that you do.**

The best source of new information is from other networks — people who run in circles different from your own. In technical terms, this is known as non-homogeneous groups.

To stimulate your creativity, it is important to tap into groups of people with whom you usually don't interact.

I offer a program called *Breakthroughs Lab*, designed to help clients work through tough problems. When I'm hired for these projects, my clients are stuck and facing an obstacle that even their most competent people can't solve. They often tell me, "We need to have all of the technical experts on this."

I ask them this — "If the technical experts haven't been able to solve the problem, then why would we have more technical experts work on the problem?"

Instead, a *Breakthroughs Lab* consists of a client and five to seven "creative catalysts" — industry experts who are also highly trained in Creative Problem-Solving. I find people who know very little or nothing about the client's problem. By nature of being new to the problem, they will have new information that the client does not have. It's sort of like coming to my holiday party, but the focus is on creating a breakthrough.

**Seek out those people that you might not usually connect with.** Talk to them. Learn from them. And if you are in Buffalo, NY in December, give me a call. There might be a party brewing.

# FYI *For Your Innovation*

## Be creative: talk to your dog.

*Ashley Cournyea was one of my creative studies graduate students at SUNY Buffalo State. Through her work, she developed techniques and tricks for fostering her own deliberate creativity. Among them? Long conversations with her pup, Tucker.*

I spend a lot of time talking to my bulldog, Tucker. Whether he understands me is not important, but how he responds is. If I am brainstorming for a personal challenge, I tell Tucker everything I come up with.

**Guess what he does?** He defers judgment. He doesn't tell me I have too many ideas. He listens to my wild and unusual ideas and he lets me use him to build on more. Tucker has never been trained in Creative Problem-Solving, **but he is a natural at following the ground rules for idea generation. I tell him what I'm thinking and he looks at me with confidence.**

This may sound silly, but some of my greatest breakthroughs have been shared with Tucker. He may not be able to respond with his own, but he never shuts mine down or says they are too crazy.

Whenever I am part of an idea generating session, I try to remember **the divergent ground rules – defer judgment, combine and build on ideas, seek wild ideas and go for quantity.** But, sometimes it's hard to follow all of them. I'll admit, sometimes I hear other people's ideas and I think to myself "Really? You think that's a good one?" And then I catch myself being judgmental. Being judgmental seems to be in our nature as humans.

Then, when I hear that a great solution came from a crazy idea early on, I'm reminded of why it is so important to be judgment-free and go for the wild and unusual. **If I spend my time thinking about why that early concept wasn't a good one, I've denied myself the opportunity to build on it.**

**Following the divergent ground rules is a way of training your brain to be creative. The more you practice, the better you will be at generating ideas that can really make a difference.**

My suggestion? Practice the divergent ground rules by talking to your dog. If you don't have a dog, think about getting one. Maybe I can train Tucker to bark every time he senses judgment.

# If a dog can follow the divergent ground rules, so can you.

INSCECTS AND MOLLUSKS IN CINEMATIC HISTORY
ONE SLUG, TWO SLUG, RED SLUG, BLUE SLUG
SLOW & STEADY THE LIFE OF A SLUG
VINTAGE
The Ugly Slugling
ABACUS
The CURIOUS INCIDENT of THE SLUG IN THE NIGHT-TIME
VINTAGE
THE YEAR OF THE SALT
SLUGS NOT DRUGS
Love Your Squish: A Guide to Slug Self-Love
flamingo
VINTAGE
SHAKESPEARE FOR SLUGS
SLUG MANUAL
CATCHER IN THE SLIME
MOLLUSK MANIFESTO
VERSO
SLUGS AND HUGS
50 SHADES OF SLIME
review
SLUG STUFF FOR DUMMIES
Human Behaviors: What Are They Thinking?
EVERYTHING
A NEW VIEW OF SOCIETY
YOUR BEST SHELL
The Perio
A SLUGS GUIDE TO BASEBALL
Shells, Sidewalks, and Other Saf
THE SECRET LIFE OF SLUG
The Metamorphosis
Slime and Prejudice
The trails we leave behind
THE MISO SOUP
The Oxford Book of Slug Short Stories
NO HANDS, NO FEET, NO PROBLEM!
MY TIME TO SLIME! A GUIDE TO LASTING SL
Mollusks on the Moon
Powder
FEAR THE BEER

# FYI *For Your Innovation*
## Don't be a slug.

Dr. Donna Hamlin at Rensselaer Polytechnic Institute did a study on the reading habits of scientists. She grouped the scientists into three categories. The first group was labeled "innovative." These scientists exhibited the highest creative productivity as measured by patents.

The second group was labeled "productive." These scientists were known for being technically proficient.

The third group was labeled "slugs." They were neither innovative nor productive.

Dr. Hamlin found that "slugs" read almost nothing. The "productive" scientists read almost exclusively in their field, while the "innovative" scientists (who were not always as technically up-to-date as their "productive" colleagues) read in a variety of fields. In fact, a great deal of the latter group's reading was outside of their area of expertise. These scientists read everything — from science fiction to technical journals, from *Popular Mechanics* to *Psychology Today* — and therefore held a diverse storehouse of information from which to generate new concepts.

A friend of mine, who is a leader in a food service organization, tells the young college graduates who work with him, "If you want to find out what's going on in the food service industry today, read *Restaurant Business* or *Food and Wine* magazine. But if you want to find out what's going to be going on in this field in the future, read *Rolling Stone, Wired* or *Entrepreneur.*"

In other words, you can read all the technical stuff in your field to find out what's going on. But to spot the trends of the future and to get new information, you need to read **outside** of your area.

Don't have time to read? Then listen to podcasts and audio books. But don't choose topics that focus solely on your business. Consciously look for topics in which you might be peripherally interested. Look for subjects that you are curious about. If you are listening in your car, keep your phone handy to record those new insights *(no texting!)*

Be ready for those new ideas to surface. You never know when you are going to create in a flash!

# FYI *For Your Innovation*

## The secret to lifetime creativity.
## Get off your butt and do something.

**"You are never too old to set another goal or dream a new dream."** *C. S. Lewis*

Creativity is usually associated with something novel and new; aging is often associated with things that are traditional and old fashioned. Creativity involves flexibility, adaptability, and openness to new ideas; aging is linked to inflexibility, dependence and outdated thinking. **Not for Ruth.**

Ruth began playing the piano at eight years old. She remembers the day when her dad drove into their farm yard with an old piano in the back of his farm truck that he had purchased at an auction.

When Ruth was 15, the organist at her family's church resigned. Before she knew it, her father had volunteered her for the job, and she had to wing it. "It wasn't easy those first few years." she said. "Sometimes I had a hard time matching the words to the music because all of the words were in German, and I didn't speak German."

Ruth was organist for over 100 weddings and 100 funerals between 1943 and 1997. She even played for the weddings of children of couples whose weddings she played for earlier in her career. She formally resigned from her full-time organist position in 1997, but she still ties on her organ shoes when there is a need. That's over 70 years performing as an organist.

In 2012, she came out of musical retirement to start a women's choir for the church. "I just thought we needed it. There was a choir loft and no choir. It just didn't seem right."

Ruth didn't only contribute musically to the church. She also taught children's Sunday School. In 1973, she was the first woman to be the president of her church's leadership council.

While raising her family in rural Colorado, Ruth canned fruits and vegetables, grew a large garden and helped her husband, Chuck, breed sheep. She was particularly busy during lambing season when she and Chuck spent long nights in the cold Colorado winter in the sheep barn helping distressed ewes give birth. Throughout her life, Ruth has been a doer, a mover and a changemaker in the lives of those around her. This type of approach and habit building keeps us mentally nimble, ready to generate new ideas and solutions.

In addition to her love of music, she is an avid quilter, was a school photographer and even took calligraphy classes. Her quilting "body of work" includes over 200 quilted pieces.

In addition to making quilts, she served as coordinator for Project Linus for 12 years. Project Linus distributes handmade quilts and blankets to hospitalized children in Northern Colorado. When she was coordinator, she picked up blankets, washed them, labeled them and delivered the blankets to local hospitals. During her time with Project Linus, she distributed over 100 blankets and quilts to sick children.

In 2004, Ruth's husband of 52 years was killed in a car accident. One might expect tragedy to slow down the creative process, or at least reduce creative productivity. But for Ruth, her creative productivity actually increased.

"I didn't know what to do with myself. It was really hard. I had all of this extra time. After Chuck died, I came across this pattern that we bought years ago when Chuck and I stopped at a quilt shop in Estes Park, CO. It was for stuffed bears. I decided to make bears out of Chuck's old clothes. I made bears for my daughter and my son. I also made pillow tops out of his old ties."

Ruth's memorial bears became so popular that she made 10 more out of the clothes of relatives and friends that had passed away.

Dr. Jennifer Gippel, who researches creativity and aging, has identified the following **essential ingredients for aging creatively:**

Imagination Although we slow down as we get older, our ability to imagine something new and different is ever-present. One way to stimulate imagination is to **deliberately do something new every day.**

Attitude A person can choose to **pursue new ideas and new ways of doing things.** Choose to view unexpected or undesired outcomes as enrichment — experiences to learn from — rather than failures.

**Knowledge** Knowledge and experience are the fuel for creativity. Knowledge grows with age. Follow your expertise and passion to learn more and continue to gain experiences, even in later years.

**Environment** The spaces where we spend time affect creativity. Surround yourself with people who support your ideas. Make a place to be creative, and design it so that it inspires your creative thinking. (Ruth has a sewing room chock full of material and patterns. She has an organ, a piano and stacks of music in her music room at home.)

**Time** Time is essential for creative thought. One of the things that older people often have is time. Use that time to follow your passions and even look for new ones.

According to Dr. Gippel, "As long as our cognitive function is intact, aging itself does not deny us any of the vital attributes and resources necessary to find creative solutions to our problems. **Creativity is largely an inner resource we can foster at any age.**"

Ruth's advice for living a long and creatively productive life: "Get involved with your church or other organizations. Join a club. Always have a project in mind. I usually have two or three projects going at one time. I alternate between three sewing machines and each one is for a different project. **Don't just sit around on your butt and do nothing.**"

Like our physical bodies, our creativity muscles need practice to thrive – and that doesn't mean just for artistic creativity. This includes the tools we need for creative problem solving on the job and in our day-to-day life.

Leaders, how does this relate to you? In our culture of youthful emphasis and focus on cutting edge resources, remember that **innovation and creativity thrives when it comes from a variety of perspectives, ages and backgrounds.** Don't discount your seasoned employees' contributions. Their experience is invaluable.

By the way, Ruth is my mother. I'm a lucky guy, with her as my example for a lifetime of creativity. Thank you, Mom!

STEP 3

# DEVELOP SOLUTIONS

Polish your ideas and get them ready for action.

Typically you will find yourself with a number of ideas that come together to create your solution. But before you're ready to implement, the concept will need refining. In this stage of the Creative Problem-Solving process, you will take the ideas you generated and develop your concepts into an actionable solution.

## In this chapter, we will:

- Use the PPCo technique to evaluate and build ideas
- Find a way to infuse creativity at any level of an organization
- Learn how failure drives innovation

Develop Solutions: PPCo Video 11/PDFs

createinaflashbook.com

Well initially, I'm always a little bit reluctant to get into a {new} process. I like to have guarantees. So, there's a risk factor involved, but it's a healthy risk factor. It can really open you up to possibilities that you would never have imagined.

Innovation in the Church
with Fr. Jack Ledwon, Ph.D.

*Pastor, St. Joseph University Parish*
*Buffalo, NY*

It has been my experience that when it comes to the stage of the Creative Problem-Solving process in which ideas are evaluated and refined, people often confuse refinement with criticism.

"Let's find what is wrong with our idea so we don't make a mistake."

We are going to take a different approach to evaluating ideas. Using a technique called PPCo, we will consciously determine the strengths of each idea **before** we determine its weaknesses.

Think about this. If you have done a good job of generating ideas, it makes absolutely no sense to pick an idea and talk about why it **won't** work. You invested the time generating those ideas in the first place, now it is important to take a structured, conscious approach to the evaluation of your ideas.

**You walk into my *Principles of Creativity* classroom. Projected on the screen in the front of the room is a diagram of a new jet. I ask your class to comment on the design. Here is what your classmates say:**

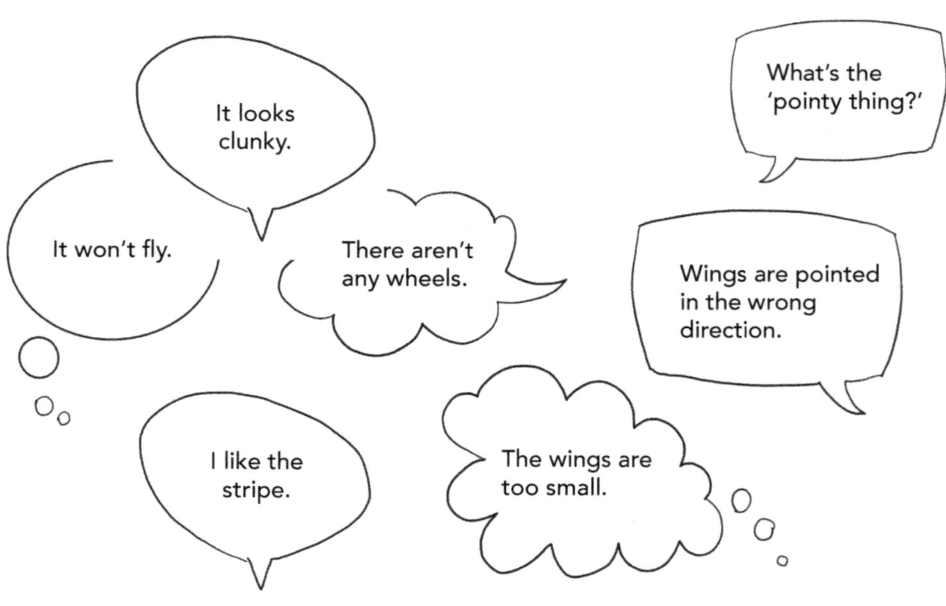

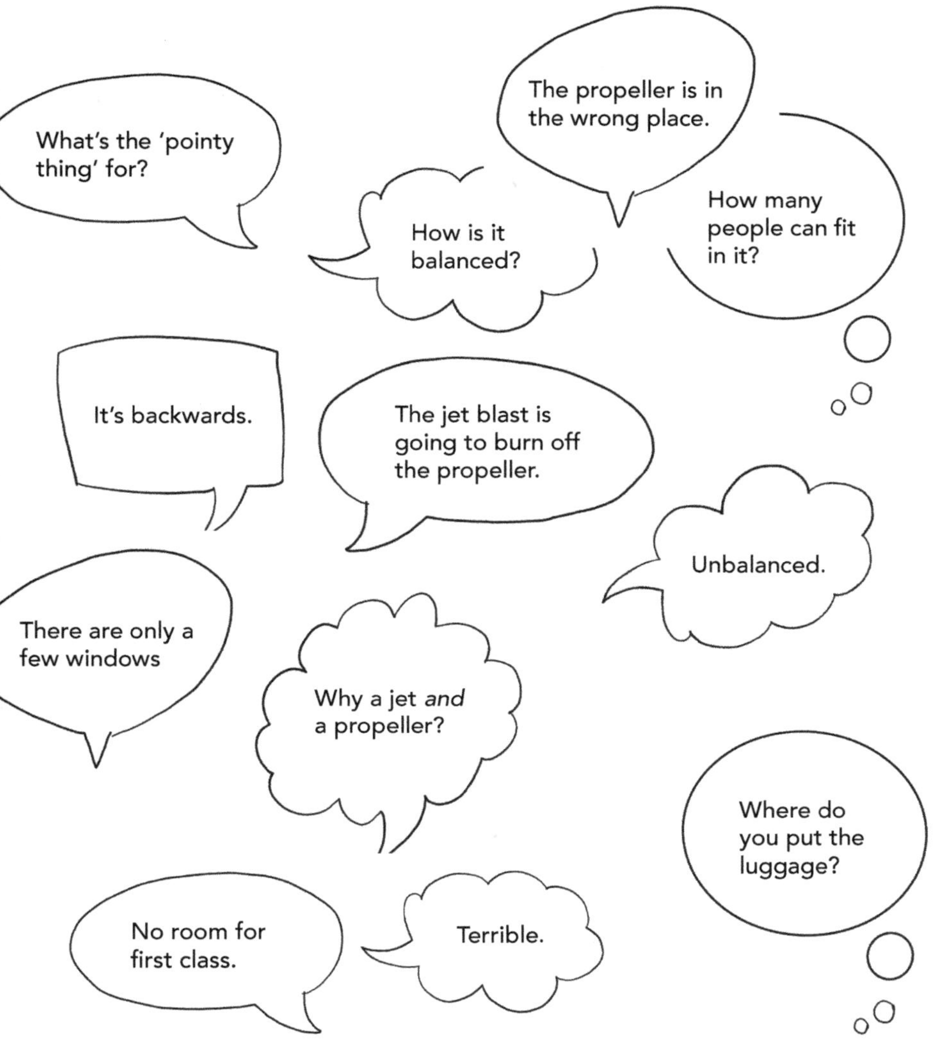


I have been tallying your comments on a legal pad. When I turn the pad around so that you can see it, here is what you see:

**The most responses? You got it. *Criticisms.***

**Notice — I asked the class to comment on the design, not to *criticize* the design.**

Negative
Questions
Positive

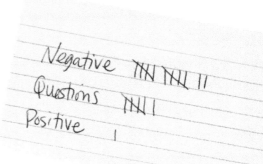

Aeronautical buffs know that this plane really does fly. It is the Lear Fan 2100 and it made its first flight in January 1981. It is made almost entirely of composite materials, which weigh half as much as aluminum. The Lear Fan is faster and more economical than conventionally-made business jets and turboprops. Only three Lear Fan airplanes were made, but the knowledge gained in composite technology has revolutionized the field of aviation.

More interesting than our unusual plane is the next question. What would have happened if I had taken your class' comments and modified the design according to their comments? What would I have?

**The same traditional airplane.**

**The Lear Fan 2100 is what new ideas look like.**

New ideas look a little strange. They seem a little odd. Sometimes we don't know all the information about the idea. And the knee jerk reaction to innovation is — **kill it!**

When asked to comment on a design, the overwhelming majority of responses from most groups or audiences are criticisms. So, how can we deal with this?

Enter, the PPCo technique.
PPCo stands for Pluses, Potentials, Concerns and Overcome concerns.

After you have generated lots of ideas and then selected the best ideas for solving a problem, PPCo can help you to evaluate to *build* the ideas rather than destroying them in the process of evaluation. Here's how.

**Start by stating the idea you want to develop in the form of an 'idea phrase,'** beginning with the words, "What I see myself doing...." Then, follow these steps.

**1. List at least three good things about the idea.**
These three traits are the **pluses** of the idea. The strengths or positive aspects of the concept. What's good about the idea, at face value, right now.

**2. List the potentials.** Potentials are spinoffs, speculations, or possible future gains that might result if the idea were implemented. These are the results it might create. Of course, potentials can be either positive or negative. But if the potentials point out a major concern that may prevent the idea from being implemented, they should be dealt with as concerns. Phrase potentials beginning with the phrase, "It might..."

**3. List the concerns about the idea.**
Concerns must be worded as a creative question if this technique is to work. Creative questions begin with the words, "How to..." or "How might...." When the concerns are phrased like a creative question, your mind recognizes them as something that can be solved and almost immediately begins to generate ideas for overcoming that concern. For example, if the concern is that the idea will cost too much, phrase your concern as "How to reduce the cost?" or "How to find the money to develop the idea?" By phrasing concerns in this way, you can generate ideas to overcome the concern, strengthen the concept, and increase its chances for acceptance. This is a positive, proactive approach to evaluating and building ideas.

**4. Overcome your concerns about the idea.**
After you have listed your concerns, generate ways to overcome each one of them, one concern at a time.

**TIP**

Choose a difficult concern to overcome first. Sometimes when people tackle their toughest concern first, other concerns evaporate.
As a result of overcoming the concerns about the idea, the idea gets better, more refined and is often ready to be implemented.

# Back to the Classroom.
## Let's try PPCo on the Lear Fan design.

### First the pluses of the design.

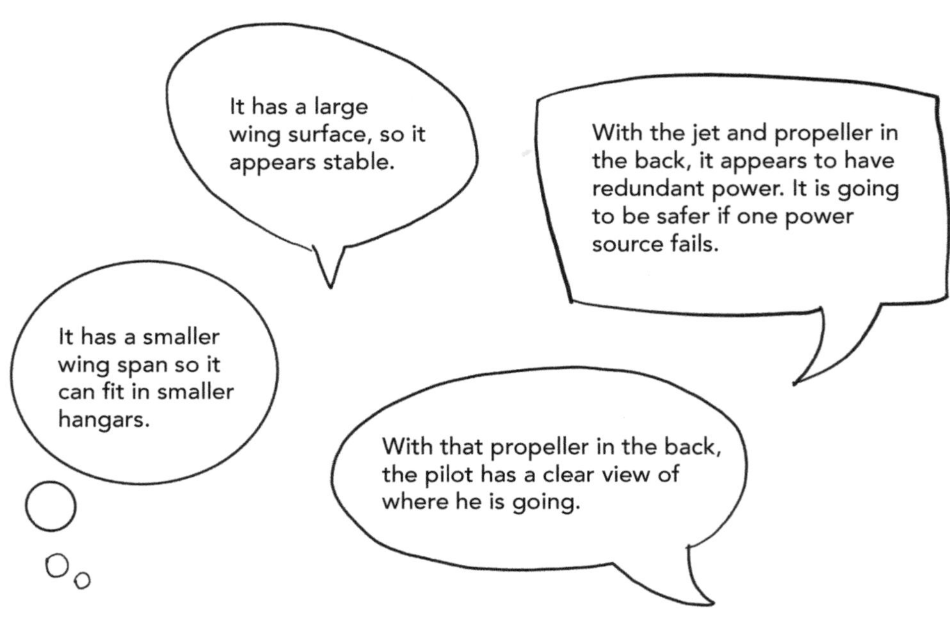

It has a large wing surface, so it appears stable.
With the jet and propeller in the back, it appears to have redundant power. It is going to be safer if one power source fails.
It has a smaller wing span so it can fit in smaller hangars.
With that propeller in the back, the pilot has a clear view of where he is going.


### Next, the potentials.

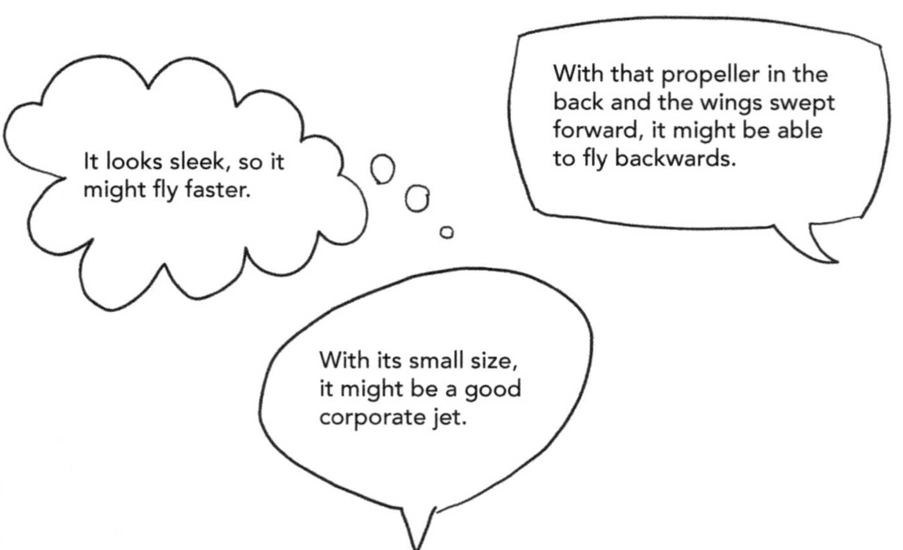

It looks sleek, so it might fly faster.
With that propeller in the back and the wings swept forward, it might be able to fly backwards.
With its small size, it might be a good corporate jet.

## Now for the concerns.

No idea is perfect, but remember – **we'll word the concern as a question**, not as a statement that blocks your thinking. For example, one concern might be: **"Will it fly?"** Reworded as a creative question, the concern becomes:

"How to pre-test the design?"

Here are a few more:

**"People might be reluctant to buy the plane because it appears so radical."**

"How to convince people to buy this new design?"

**"That plane looks so crazy, it might be difficult to fly."**

"How to train people to fly the plane?"

This is the PPC part of the technique. The next part of the technique is designed to overcome the concerns, one concern at a time.

## Concern #1

### How to pre-test the design?

"Build a model and put it in a wind tunnel."
"Design it on a computer and use computer simulations to test it."
"Look for similar designs on the market that we could learn from."
"Talk to pilots and get their ideas before we begin design work."
"Talk to potential customers and find out what they think."
"Ask aeronautical engineers for ideas to improve the design."
"Make a remote-control model."

## Concern #2

### How to convince people to buy this new design?

"Take it to air shows and fly it in exhibitions."
"Do a video from the perspective of a passenger in the plane."
"Show how it is similar to other planes that people are used to."
"Publish statistics on its safety record."
"Get testimonials from people who have flown on it."

## Concern #3

### How to train people to fly the plane?

"Use virtual reality simulations."
"Use flight simulators."
"Talk to pilots and get their suggestions on flying it."
"Have the designer fly the plane."
"Have flight engineers fly the plane first."

As a result of doing Pluses, Potentials, Concerns and Overcoming the concerns, a number of things begin to happen to the idea.

**The initial idea gets better.**

**It becomes more feasible.**

**You begin to see the steps you might need to take to implement the idea.**

PPCo helps you to analyze and improve ideas, instead of just dismissing a solution or concept that seems difficult, crazy or impossible. As we overcome each one of our concerns, it helps to raise the 'threshold of acceptability' of the idea. The PPCo technique helps to make an idea better and stronger. By phrasing concerns like a creative question, we open our minds to come up with ideas for overcoming those obstacles.

After analyzing an idea using Pluses, Potentials and Concerns, you may determine that the solution may not be feasible or the right thing for right now. That's all a part of the process. Now, you know that you have fully explored the idea with PPCo instead of dismissing it outright, and you've identified the specific reasons why it's not the right thing to implement at the moment. You can always return to an idea later.

**You can respect an idea without implementing it.**

# The toy designers.

## Great at creating ideas. Great at destroying ideas.

Very early in my career I was hired by the toy design group at Fisher-Price to do a creativity workshop at their annual toy design conference. This is the conference where they make decisions on which toys will be produced two years in the future.

The meeting was held at a beautiful conference center in Niagara on the Lake, in Ontario, Canada. I arrived the day before the session, checked into a beautiful room that overlooked Lake Ontario, and set off to join the group for dinner.

As I got closer to the private room that was set aside for our dinner, I heard laughter, shouting and found a group of people having a terrific time.

I had a marvelous dinner with these folks. These people were the epitome of what you might expect from highly creative toy designers — intelligent, expressive and a little zany.

**They scared the hell out of me.**

As I went back to my room that night I thought about slinking away under the cover of darkness. What was *I* going to teach these people? By their profession, and by their very nature, they were already creative.

It was a long, restless night.

When I started the session the next morning, they were ready for me. Generating ideas for these folks was a breeze. They had more ideas than any group I had ever worked with. Creating ideas was nothing new for them.

The PPCo technique was the breakthrough for this group.

That afternoon, as was the tradition for these meetings, the members of the group presented their new toy ideas. When I talked to the vice president of this division later, he told me that this part of the conference usually resulted in a blood bath.

Designers would present their toy designs and would usually get destroyed. Just as these people were highly skilled at generating ideas, they were also highly skilled at destroying ideas. When colleagues presented their designs, the group easily came up with all the reasons why those designs weren't going to work.

**This time, it was different.**

This time the designers used the Pluses, Potentials, Concerns technique to present and evaluate their concepts. The vice president told me this was the most well-run and productive session ever held at Fisher-Price's toy design conference. He also told me that as a result of this session, they got more, and better, toy designs in the product pipeline than in any previous year.

**The designers left this meeting with suggestions that refined and strengthened their designs, as opposed to the traditional result of total carnage.**

# PPCo in action.

## You want to infuse creativity in your organization and the boss isn't interested? Be like Dick Donovan.

**Scenario:** You work in a large organization. Top management is lukewarm to the idea of launching a full-scale innovation initiative throughout the company.

If you really believe that it is important for your team to be creative, then follow Dick Donovan's example. Take Nike's advice and "just do it."

Dick recently retired from his position as vice president of business continuity management of a very large bank in Buffalo, NY. The team that Dick led was responsible for resumption of business activities in the event that they were significantly disrupted. Natural disasters, data recovery, systems failures — Dick's team was on the job. It was a small, highly-trained team of six to eight employees.

Dick's team demonstrated that Creative Problem-Solving works on a small scale.

Dick reflected on when he was promoted to team leader. "My staff meetings consisted of the six people in my department talking about the future and the things that were going on in the organization. We very rarely had a formal 'meeting'."

"There wasn't much structure to these gatherings," he explained. "When we would start to work on a new business area, that's when my team would really open up."

"***But*** — to get people to open up you have to start with the basic consideration of what people want." Dick emphasized. "People don't want to be criticized. People don't want to be told to shut up. People want to know that when they put forward an idea everyone is listening, regardless of where they sit in the organization."

"Even though everybody knew that I was the team leader, I just tried to be another voice within the group, not the big manager."

"We really didn't do any formal Creative Problem-Solving training, but I was taking graduate courses in creative studies at SUNY Buffalo State. When I learned something pretty cool in class, I would come back to work the next day and we would talk about it."

What really stuck with the group?

"One of the things that they loved was PPCo (Pluses, Potentials, Concerns and Overcome concerns.) I would tell them, 'We are going to PPCo this idea. But don't give me the concerns first. Let's move those concerns down the line a bit.' We can't be concerned about something that doesn't exist yet."

**Dick's department flourished.** When the bank conducted employee engagement surveys, the business continuity team was consistently among the most engaged in the organization. The group was high functioning, and Dick frequently received transfer requests from employees in other departments.

"Other than that, we really didn't get a lot of formal recognition from the larger organization," according to Dick. "Recognition for our team was internal. We knew how we worked together, and that was good enough. I am retired now, but I will always remember that as my best work experience."

So, there it is. **You don't have to train the whole organization.** *You can nurture creative pockets of light in your organization,* just like Dick did.

# Make the right mistakes.

## From "trial and error" to "trial and *learn.*"

A music director once told me that when he rehearsed, he preferred the musicians to make mistakes confidently. He wanted the mistakes to be big and loud so he would notice them quickly, provide coaching and help the ensemble improve. In the end, the concert audience would only hear the orchestra at their best.

**When you're working toward a solution, don't avoid mistakes on the path.** There are plenty of "right" mistakes that can be made. In fact, the greatest mistake possible is trying to avoid making mistakes at all. Avoidance can cause stress, worry about failing and can hinder creativity. Like the music director, I recommend that you adopt the attitude that mistakes can help you improve and make progress.

Consider the phrase, "trial and error." Error, in this context, is not a negative word. It is a sign that adjustment is needed. Making "good" mistakes has driven invention, product development, scientific discovery and the creative process for hundreds of years. Tests are run, results are noted, changes are made. The process begins again, and eventually the outcomes improve.

Still not ready to embrace mistakes? Look at it another way: a mistake is a result you didn't anticipate. So think, "What can I LEARN...?" **Challenge yourself to change your thinking from "trial and error" to "trial and *learn.*"** Think about it: if you were learning to ride a bike and fell down, would you call that a mistake and punish yourself? Or would you get up, learn from the fall and get moving again? Ups and downs are just part of the process!

Because it is so important to be open to making mistakes, I bring this concept to the forefront during creativity training programs. I give the group permission to make 30 mistakes. If they make 30, I give them 30 more. It is amazing to see a group relax, laugh and participate when they know I will not criticize them.

If you want to bring more creativity into your work and personal life, embrace the mistake quota. Give yourself permission to make lots of "right" mistakes. **Make 'em big and make 'em loud.** Laugh about them and learn from them. That way, when it's show time, you are ready to give your best!

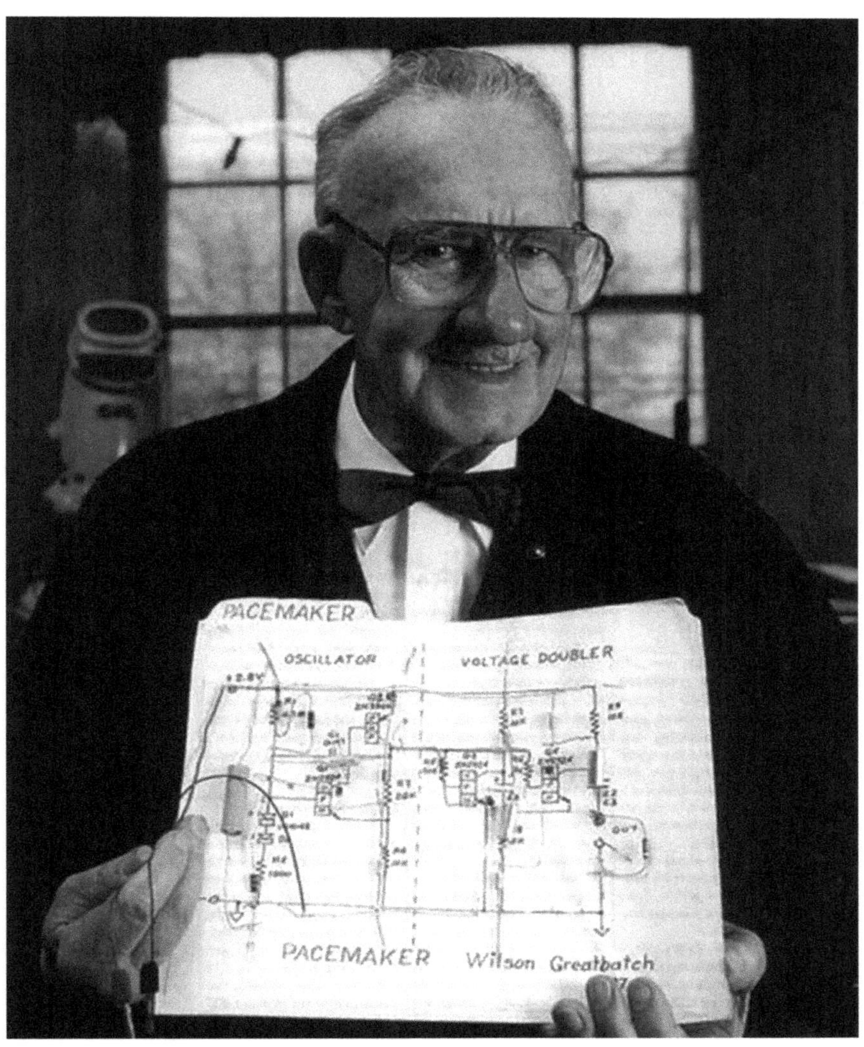


**"I look forward to failure as a learning experience. Nine out of ten things that I work on fail, but the one that works pays for the other nine."**

Dr. Wilson Greatbatch, inventor of the implantable cardiac pacemaker.

STEP 4

# PLAN FOR ACTION

Great innovation requires a great plan.

The Plan for Action stage is crucial. You generated lots of different ways to clarify the problem, and then you generated lots of ideas for solving that problem. Now is the time to put your solutions into action.

## In this chapter, we will:

- Use a check list to assure successful implemention of innovations
- Learn how to develop an action plan to implement your solution
- Review a strategy for generating and focusing specific action steps

Generating Action Steps Video 12/PDF
Create Your Action Plan Video 13
CPS: The Whole Process Video 14

createinaflashbook.com

Your class changed the way we think about things. It was like you hit a beehive with a stick. A ton of ideas flew out into the room. You helped us bring those ideas together and focus them into an actionable plan.

Innovation in Medicine
with Dr. Robert Gatewood

*Cardiology hospitalist,*
*Buffalo, NY*

# Plan for action.

You may have the most amazing vision or goal in the world. You have taken the time to carefully redefine that goal with lots of creative questions. You have groundbreaking ideas for solving those creative questions resulting in elegantly refined ideas.

But if you don't do anything with your ideas, all of this work has just been an academic exercise.

To create your vision, you've navigated the Creative Problem-Solving process, but you haven't yet experienced the joy and the challenges of putting your idea into action.

You have deprived the world of your creative breakthrough.

It is now your responsibility to share your idea with the world.

**"A fair idea *implemented* is better than a good idea kept on the polishing wheel."**

*Alex Osborn*

Don't sell yourself short by telling yourself that your idea isn't any good. How will you know for sure until you have taken that first step? How will you make the world a better place until you share your solution with others?

This is not the time in the creative process to wimp out.

**This is the time to be BOLD.**
**This is the time for ACTION.**

In his classic book *Diffusion of Innovations,* Everett Rogers studied how new ideas get adopted into the world.

According to Rogers,"An *innovation* is an idea, practice, or object that is perceived as new by an individual or other unit of adoption." In other words, an innovation does not have to be tangible like a smart phone or a personal computer. An innovation can be farmers adopting hybrid corn seed, communities adopting the use of solar panels, developing nations adopting family planning or a city adopting ride sharing like Uber or Lyft.

## You dramatically increase the chances of your idea being adopted, used, put into practice or sold if you can show the following:

Relative advantage is the degree to which an innovation is perceived as better than the product or practice it replaces. The greater the perceived relative advantage of an innovation, the more rapid its rate of adoption is going to be.

Compatibility is the degree to which an innovation is consistent with the existing values, past experiences and needs of potential adopters. An idea that is not compatible with the prevalent values and norms of a society will not be adopted as rapidly as an innovation that is compatible.

Complexity is the degree to which an innovation is perceived as difficult to understand. This is what you DON'T want. The key is to make the idea easy to understand.

Trial ability is the degree to which an innovation may be experimented with on a limited basis. New ideas that can be tried on the installment plan will generally be adopted more quickly than innovations that are not divisible. Think: test driving a car. Can you try before you buy?

Observability is the degree to which the results of an innovation are visible to others. The easier it is for potential adopters to see the results of an innovation, the more likely they are to adopt it.

# How to make things happen.

## Rogers' *Diffusion of Innovation* characteristics in action.

Last summer, I replaced the original 73-year-old windows in my house, repaved the crumbling driveway and gutted a basement room that had become the final resting place for six mice. Yuck.

I thought I was finished with my renovations until I clicked on Phil Colarusso's website. Phi is a lighting designer in Western New York who lights houses and landscapes. He had completed work for friends, and when I saw the beautiful work that he does, I couldn't resist.

When Phil stopped by to give me an estimate, he asked questions that were different from what I expected. He asked what kind of wine I liked, whether I want to light my home for myself or for how I appear to others, and even how I want to feel when I pull in my driveway at night. He asked those questions so he could understand how best to capture the ambiance, mood and emotions I wanted my home to evoke.

About a week later, Phil dropped off a proposal that included lighting the front of the house, the side yard and my back yard. My budget was getting tight from all of those other major expenses, so I couldn't afford the entire project.

Phil suggested that we do the lighting in phases. "I recommend that we light the house first. And, I happen to have a light that I used in my showroom before I remodeled it. I can include it at no charge for your side yard." he suggested.

That worked for me. And the first night that I walked out to the street and looked up at the house, I was hooked.

**Let's see how well Phil did on Everett Rogers' characteristics of innovations.**

**Relative advantage.**
How much better is the innovation than the product it replaces?
*Phil's lighting is so much better than stringing Christmas lights in my trees.* ✓

**Compatibility**
Is this consistent with your values or past experiences?
*Phil's questions made sure my lighting was right for me.* ✓

**Complexity**
Is the idea easy to understand? Complexity is what we **don't** want.
*I liked Phil's work for my friends. I knew what Phil could do. Simple.* ✓

**Trial ability.**
Think: Can you try before you buy?
*Phil let me try a piece of the project before he did the whole thing.* ✓

**Observability.**
Can you see it?
*Easy, look at my yard!* ✓

**As I reviewed this checklist, I think Phil got them all. No wonder I am saving up to light the rest of my property.**

# Using questions to get your idea adopted.

You used the Creative Problem-Solving process to help you to redefine your goal, **and** you used the Creative Problem-Solving process to generate lots of ideas. Now, you can also use the process to generate and select the actions that will help you systematically and deliberately implement your solution.

To help you generate those actions, follow the guidelines for divergent thinking. Except this time, instead of generating creative questions or lots of ideas, the goal is to generate lots of potential actions that could be taken to implement your new idea.

Use the following guidelines to generate action steps:

1. **Defer judgment.**
2. **Strive for quantity.**
3. **Seek wild and unusual actions.**
4. **Build on other actions.**

Review those potential action steps and select the most important ones that you will need to take to get your solution implemented. Build them into a plan that identifies:

1. The action you want to take.
2. Who is going to do the action.
3. When the action is going to be done.
4. Who you'll need support from or who you need to report to as you move forward.

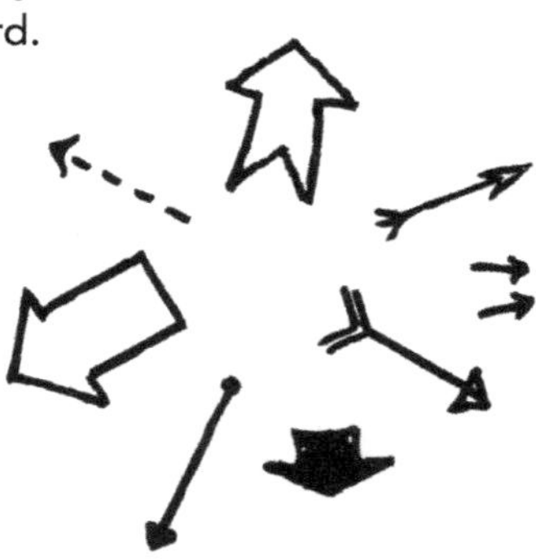

## Here are some questions to help you generate your potential action steps.

If you generate three potential actions for each of the following questions you will have 58 ways to get your idea adopted.

1. How might you make your solution easy to understand?
2. How might you demonstrate that your solution is better than what is currently being done?
3. How might you demonstrate the advantages of your solution?
4. What might you do to gain acceptance of your solution?
5. How might you earn others' enthusiasm for your idea?
6. How might you demonstrate that your solution is consistent with the values of the people you want to adopt it?
7. In what special places or locations might you implement your solution? What are some places or locations to avoid?
8. How might someone sample your solution before committing?
9. What special times might you implement your solution?
10. What might be all of the things that could assist you when implementing your solution?
11. What might be all of the things that could resist you when implementing your solution?
12. What might be all the ways to overcome resistance?
13. What additional resources might help you to implement your idea (e.g., individuals, groups, materials, money)?
14. How might you pre-test your solution?
15. What first steps might you take to put your solution into action?
16. What other actions might you take to implement your solution?

# A great plan can change a nation.

Dr. John Cabra is a professor of creative studies at SUNY Buffalo State. In 2004, John met a student named Myo Thant, a Burmese refugee who had been driven out of Myanmar due to national unrest. Despite his experience, Myo Thant remained fiercely committed to his home country, inspiring John to establish a study abroad program in Myanmar. The country was in turmoil at the time, but he set his sights on building the program for the future in hopes of making an impact on a nation in need.

By 2016, the majority of Myanmar had stabilized and John Cabra began sharing the idea of the program with the university community.
The excitement was palpable, but he faced several hurdles.

**Community acceptance** The concern for student safety was immediate. Northern Myanmar was experiencing ethnic cleansing - a genocide. John's program was designed to stay only in areas of the country that were considered safe for travel, but parents and administrators still voiced concerns.

**Enrollment** John was working to attract student interest in the program, which would ultimately determine its viability.

**Funding** Every new program needs cash to make it go, and this was no exception.

John hatched a plan for action. He used the action planning questions to build his strategy to create the Myanmar program. Most of the time you don't need to use all 16. In this instance we'll explore six.

**How might you demonstrate that your solution is better than what is currently being done?** John built his program to be tailored to individual students' educational expertise, creating a custom in-the-field experience for each participant that would also provide benefit to Burmese organizations in need. Paired with the cultural exposure of working in Myanmar, the program was undeniably unique for students, and attractive because they could build their own experience.

**What might you do to you gain acceptance of your solution?**
When faced with hesitancy regarding safety, John was able to use outside resources. The US State Department had assessed the majority of Myanmar as safe for travel. To confirm the safety of the area, Myo Thant traveled to the intended study areas and returned with positive news about the state of the nation.

**How might you earn others' enthusiasm for your idea?**
John strategically worked with faculty who had expressed interest in this initiative, and other colleagues whose students stood to gain from the program's approval.

To recruit students, John spoke in classes and gatherings on campus. He presented Myo Thant's story along with an invitation to join the planned trip to Myanmar.

**How might you demonstrate that your solution is consistent with the values of the people you want to adopt it?**
Within Buffalo State's vision is the university's intention to be a leader as a "cross-culturally competent community dedicated to developing leaders for an increasingly global society." By demonstrating that his program was aligned with the school's own commitment to global activism, John was able to garner support from within the university.

**What might be all of the things that might assist you when implementing your solution?** Making allies who also believed in globally-relevant programming was key in John's plan. He worked with faculty who had experience with study abroad programs, and others who had faced concerned stakeholders in the past.

**What additional resources might help you to implement your idea (e.g. individuals, groups, materials, money)?**
Once acceptance and enrollment goals had been achieved, the expense of travel became a hurdle. John began sharing Myo Thant's story, which resulted in several donors stepping forward to fill the funding gap.

John Cabra's Myanmar study abroad program was an undeniable success - in Burmese communities, and for Buffalo State. In the first year alone, students were able to work with members of parliament to improve governance of budgetary processes, contribute in Burmese schools, and work toward creating a mental health clinic. Now entering its third cycle, the program is recognized for creating meaningful change in a country with great need.

**All of this was possible because John knew how to create a plan for action.**

Think about your workplace. When do you need to put an idea into action? By asking just six of the 16 action-planning questions, John created a strong plan that made a big difference in a tough situation. The lesson? Plan it out before you roll it out and pave the road to success.

# CREATE IN A FLASH

## GM Invests $1.50, Saves $50k a Week

*Cue the dinner bell - this recipe is a winner.*

A ring gear is not a glamorous product. You could go through your entire life not knowing what a ring gear is. But you wouldn't get very far. A ring gear changes the direction of power in rear-wheel drive vehicles. If you have a rear-wheel drive car or truck in your garage, you have a ring gear in your garage.

General Motors makes ring gears for its vehicles at its engine plant in Tonawanda, NY. The gears are mechanically pressed with a die — a hot, doughnut-shaped piece of metal goes into the press, 50 tons of pressure is applied, a hot ring gear comes out. *Voila.*

Except at the GM plant a number of years ago, the ring gears began getting stuck in the die.

To prevent the gears from getting stuck, an operator would put a slab of grease on the die. This solved their original problem, but created another. The grease residue solidified, and the die would break. Problem #2. The big one.

***Each die cost $5,000. The plant was breaking about ten dies a week. A $50,000 loss weekly. $200,000 a month.*** ***Big problem.***

Meanwhile Austin Scaccia, Associate Administrator for Personnel and Safety at the plant, had taken several creative studies classes at SUNY Buffalo State. He began to apply what he learned about creativity at work.

His friend Nathan Bliss was the United Auto Workers Problem Solving Training Coordinator. Nathan became interested in what Austin was sharing with him about creativity. Together, they invited a few SUNY Buffalo State creative studies faculty to train some of the staff. About 40 people in the plant had been trained when the ring gear problem surfaced.

Austin and Nate decided to try out their Creative Problem-Solving skills on the ring gear problem.

One day, toward the end of a shift, they gathered together a group of people to tackle the $50,000 problem. They looked for anyone available who had been trained in Creative Problem-Solving, and rounded up ten people from various departments in the plant. Operators that worked on the presses, maintenance staff, an accountant and a couple of engineers formed the group.

**Everyone knew that the ring gear problem was a biggie.**
They stated the problem as: "How might we prevent the ring gears from getting stuck in the die?" They started generating ideas. After about 30 ideas one of the operators spoke up.

"You know, we have a sticking problem here. My wife has this vegetable product called PAM™ and when she sprays it on a pan while cooking, the food doesn't stick to the pan. Why don't we just spray the dies with PAM™?"

The group laughed, but one of the chemical engineer's eyes lit up.

"You know, PAM™ probably won't work. But Penfield Oil #108 and some #10 soap just might stop the sticking."

This idea sounded like a breakthrough.

They were so excited, they stopped the session. Half of the group went off to find the ingredients for the solution and the other half ran out to the parking lot, jumped into their Chevrolet cars and raced off to the nearest Kmart to get a spray bottle.

Upon returning, they mixed the solution — it cost about 50 cents — into a $1.00 spray bottle. They sprayed the solution onto the die.

The dies stopped breaking. **A $1.50 solution saved the plant $50,000 a week. Not a bad investment, right?**

# Let's see how well the folks at GM followed the recipe for innovation.

1. They clearly defined the problem. "How might we prevent the ring gears from getting stuck in the die?"

2. They generated lots of ideas. They came up with at least 30.

3. They used forced connections to supercharge their idea generation. PAM™ spray, a home cooking product, was the inspiration for the breakthrough to a solution for a heavy duty industrial production problem.

4. They developed their solution. It took a few tries to get the right mixture of soap and oil.

5. They put their idea into action. They sprayed the solution on the dies and the dies stopped breaking.

What else helped?

**Leadership was on board for solving the problem and using the CPS process.** Senior leadership was all over this. They needed this problem solved. $50,000 a week is a lot of money. "Local" leadership provided by Austin and Nathan was crucial in using CPS to create the breakthrough.

**Everyone in that group was trained in Creative Problem-Solving.** That's why they solved the problem in just 30 minutes instead of days or months.

That is the power of **deliberate creativity**.

That is the power of **using a tested recipe to innovate**.

That is ***creating in a flash***.

# 40 years in creativity: Lessons learned.

One reason to write a book is to share something that, deep in your heart, you are so passionate about, that means so much to you, that you can't keep it to yourself.

I want you to know that I have held nothing back in this book. As we end our time together, I would like to share with you some of the things that I have learned from my 40-year love affair with creativity.

Invest in your core principles for the sake of your employees, your product and your customers. If your company has the word "innovative" or "creative" in its vision or values statement, folks within your organization must be trained in creativity methods, with a budget that reflects those values.

To benefit from being deliberately creative, train the leadership team first. It is crucial that the top members of the organization are thoroughly trained in creativity methods so they can teach their subordinates and coach the application of creativity skills.

Stick with it. When you introduce something as different as deliberate creativity, some members in your organization will hold back and not get involved. After a year or two, your leadership team might look at the program and say, "Well, we're only getting minimal outcomes. Let's change to another program." That decision trains your workforce not to participate in company initiatives. It tells obstinate employees that if they don't participate, new efforts go away because the new initiatives have failed. Training your people to be creative on demand is a long-term investment that will serve your organization long into the future. Follow through and don't play flavor of the month.

If you believe working creatively is important but top management isn't on board, don't waste your time trying to convince them. Just do it. You can create pockets of light in your organization.

Walk the talk. As a leader, if you believe creativity is important, then you have to be creative. Show your people that it is OK to struggle with crazy ideas and to make mistakes. That it's OK to fail. Your people will watch your lead and they will follow it.

Be an example of what you are trying to teach. When someone presents you with a new idea, don't be the first person to destroy it. Look at the strengths of the idea first — remember Pluses, Potentials and Concerns?

Choose which metrics are important to your organization and use them to evaluate your success. Take care not to allow commercial innovation systems to become an end in themselves. Your success can't be guaranteed by counting the number of brainstorming sessions you are doing in a month. If you are going to use a system, have regular celebrations to showcase the specific results your people have obtained by applying creativity methods, not simply checking boxes.

Keep it simple. The methods presented in this book are my go-to creativity techniques that always work. Don't force people through some lock-step method, or overwhelm them with creativity tools just because they are cool or fun. Your people want to solve problems more effectively, they don't want to become creative process junkies. You don't need to know every part of a bicycle to ride one well.

Learn how to properly conduct a Creative Problem-Solving session from a reputable source. And yes — I'm thrilled to help!

Practice. Practice. Practice. The more you use these simple tools, the quicker you will be able to turn on your creativity at will.

## Thank you for reading my book.

I have heard it said that the way to judge a good book is if you can get an idea, just one idea that you can carry with you. In this book I'm sharing my life's work — the work I fell in love with when I was 21 years old. May I be so bold as to suggest one idea to carry with you? In the words of my philosopher farmer friend, Phil Keppler.

**"Creativity gives you hope. And that is the most important thing in life — hope."**

# About Roger

Dr. Roger Firestien has taught more people to lead the creative process than anyone else in the world. He is senior faculty and an associate professor at the Center for Applied Imagination at SUNY Buffalo State and president of Innovation Resources, Inc, an innovation consulting firm.

By applying Roger's work in creativity: Clorox solved a 77-year-old problem in 15 minutes; Mead Paper developed a world-class line of products and saved $500,000 a year; The Los Angeles Times set their vision for the future; and Western New York developed an economic development plan that was awarded one billion dollars.

Called the "Gold Standard" of creativity training by his clients, he has presented programs in creativity to over 600 organizations nationally and internationally, ranging from Fortune 500 corporations and government agencies to universities, professional associations and churches.

Roger is the author and co-author of five other books, and his expert views on creativity have been reported in *Fast Company* and *The New York Times*.

**Let's connect!** Creativity is in my soul, and I love to share it. Here's how we can create together.

**Send me your stories.** Please share your experiences using what you learned in *Create in a Flash* or the accompanying videos. Email your stories or your questions to roger@rogerfirestien.com. Your case study could feature in my next book or blog post.

**Let me help!** What we've covered in this book is just the tip of the iceberg. There are is a creative approach for every problem and I love working with folks to help them discover new avenues. Visit rogerfirestien.com and let's get to work.

I can't wait to hear from you. Really.
I *really* want to hear from you! Thank you.

# ONLINE RESOURCES

createinaflashbook.com

## Video Cooking Lessons

Intro to Creative Problem-Solving Video 1
Identify Your Goal/Wish/Challenge Video 2
Gather Data Video 3
Clarify the Problem: Creative Questions Video 4
Clarify the Problem: Why? What's Stopping Me? Video 5
Selecting the Best Problem Video 6
How to do a Warm-up Video 7
Generating Ideas: Sticky Notes + Forced Connections Video 8
Generating Ideas: Brainwriting Video 9
Selecting the Best Ideas Video 10
Develop Solutions: PPCo Video 11
Generating Action Steps Video 12
Create Your Action Plan Video 13
CPS: The Whole Process Video 14

## Printable CPS Tools & Worksheets

Creative Problem-Solving Model
Identify Your Goal/Wish/Challenge
Gather Data
Clarify the Problem: Creative Questions
Clarify the Problem: Why? What's Stopping Me?
Generating Ideas: Sticky Notes + Forced Connections
Generating Ideas: Brainwriting
Develop Solutions: PPCo
Generating Action Steps

## Applied Innovation Interview Video Series

Innovation in Economic Development with Jane Fischer
Innovation in Education with Mary Bennett
Innovation in Business with Erik Eustice
Innovation in Agriculture with Phillip Keppler
Innovation in the Church with Fr. Jack Ledwon, Ph.D.
Innovation in Medicine with Dr. Robert Gatewood

# *CREATE IN A FLASH* VIDEO CAST

**Najja Bouldin** teaches the art within the science of creativity. On this dutiful mission to ignite creativity throughout the universe, he is light and love.
*Also pictured, Najja Jr!*

**Kari D'Amico** believes that creativity is deeply woven into her life. Kari teaches creativity courses for the Center for Applied Imagination, SUNY Buffalo State.

**Phil Marks** is a creativity facilitator in deliberate creativity, innovation and change leadership. He coaches corporate leadership in long-established industries.

**Ashley Cournyea** is a high school art teacher in Buffalo, NY and a proud graduate of the creative studies master's program at SUNY Buffalo State.

**Dianne Britain** uses the Creative Problem-Solving process in her activism work to change the world for the better.

**Tamara L McMillan,** is an author and lecturer at the Center for Applied Imagination at SUNY Buffalo State and Director of CSTEP.

**Teresa Lawrence** applies tools of creativity to project management to help leaders solve challenges and leverage opportunities for maximum value-realization in their work.

**Mike Raisch** is an instructor of Creative Problem-Solving at Genesee Community College near Rochester, NY. He also facilitates the creative process to help clients take control of their environment.

**Michaelene Dawson-Globus** brings creative thinking into teaching and training, game invention and social work practice. Her mission is to help people harness creativity for positive change.

**Kirk Young** uses his creative expertise in strategy and planning at the college where he works in Jamestown, NY. Kirk uses creativity in various community initiatives and consults nationwide.

**Marcus Branch** is a graduate of the creative studies master's program at SUNY Buffalo State. He is a learning and development specialist at Delaware North Corp.

# THANK YOU

Ismet Mamnoon, Audrey Pike, Sam Insalaco, John F. Cabra, Erik Eustice, Laree Kiely, Robert Gatewood, Phillip Keppler, Mary Bennett, Suzanne Whittaker, Jack Ledwon, Jane Fischer, Alan Gozdalski, Joe Fox and Brandon Mancuso of TrainSMART Personal Fitness, Philip Colarusso, G. Douglas Reid, Judy Reid, Gina Gray, Jennifer Nahrebeski, Jerome Mach, Jacquelin Welch, my retired Chief of Staff Lois Donovan, Bill Shepard, Diane Foucar-Szocki, Gary Gorski, Sarah Thurber, Dorte Nielsen, Ken Kumiega, Dick Donovan, MaryBeth Whiting, Mike Whiting, David Schubel, Dawn Keppler, Mark Thomas, Elaine Thomas, Susan Keller-Mathers, Cyndi Burnett, Admiral Mike Fox, Gerard Puccio, Selcuk Acar, Jo Yudess, Marie Mance, Debi Johnson, Samantha Bonano, Bobby Lebel, Vic Nole, Tom Ulbrich, Bridget Horn, Mary Irwin-Scott, Alberta Certo, Andrew Lazickas, Paul O'Brien, Naomi Tinkelman, David Newman, Dan Janal, Austin Scaccia, Nathan Bliss, Lori Weise, Gary Steeves, David Kozak, MaryAnne Kozak, Sean Rowe, Jonathan Vehar, Blair Miller, Bruce Zgoda, Cathy Zgoda, Craig Liebig, Gail Liebig, D. Stephen McAuliffe, James A. Wanner, Scott R. Kempshall, Fotini Galanes, my wonderful daughter Maria Anderson, my amazing sister Judith Firestien and the forever creative, Momma Ruth Firestien.

To all of the *Create in a Flash* video cast members:
Kirk Young, Phil Marks, Teresa Lawrence, Ashley Cournyea, Mike Raisch, Kari D'Amico, Najja Bouldin, Marcus Branch, Dianne Britain, Michelene Dawson, and Tamara McMillan.

Special thanks to Chuck Firestien. God-speed Dad.
You've got some farming to do in heaven.

# END NOTES


**Chapter One – Why Create**

Kim, K. H. (2011). *The creativity crisis: The decrease in creative thinking scores on the Torrance Tests of Creative Thinking.* Creativity Research Journal, 23(4), 285-295.

Kaufman, J. C., & Beghetto, R. A. (2009). *Beyond big and little: The four c model of creativity.* Review of General Psychology, 13(1), 1-12.

Ekvall, G. (1996). *Organizational climate for creativity and innovation.* European Journal of Work and Organizational Psychology, 5(1), 105-123.

*Leaders beware if the water is calm.* Kumiega, K. personal communication, January 15, 2019.

**Chapter Two – Creativity Basics**

Firestien, R. L. (1990). *Effects of creative problem-solving training on communication behaviors in small groups.* Small Group Research, 21(4), 507-521.

**Chapter Three – Clarify the Problem**

*The Corian Story.* Weppler, P. personal communication, August 1992.

Wedell-Wedellsborg, T. (2017). *Are you solving the right problems?* Harvard Business Review, 95(1), 76-83.

Ackoff, R. L. & Greenberg, D. (2008). *Turning Learning Right Side Up.* Upper Saddle River, NJ: Wharton School Publishing.

Weise, L. (2015). First home, forever home: *How to start and run a shelter intervention program.* CreateSpace Independent Publishing Platform.

Ogana, Yoko. (2003). *The housekeeper and the professor.* New York, Picador.

The Why/What's Stopping technique is based on the work of Parnes, S., Noller, R., & Biondi, A. (1977). Guide to Creative Action. New York, NY: Scribners.

**Chapter Four – Generate Ideas**

The Nike Waffle Trainer origin story was written by Nielsen, D., & Thurber, S. (2016). *The secret of the highly creative thinker.* Amsterdam, The Netherlands. BIS Publishers.

Osborn, A. F. (1953). *Applied imagination: Principles and procedures of creative thinking.* New York: Charles Scribner's Sons.

*Don't get fat. Get a facilitator.* Fischer, J. & Yerico, T. Personal communication May 17, 2017.

Bathtub drone by Johannes and Philip Mickenbecker. [Video] Retrieved from www.youtube.com/watch?v=EQK9m_OBVgY

The toy Whac-a-mole mattelgames.com/en-us/kids/whac-mole

Gippel, J. (2017). *Life-long creativity: Changing the narrative of aging and retirement.* Unpublished master's thesis, State University of New York, Buffalo New York.

**Chapter Five – Develop Solutions**

The Museum of flight (2016). Lear Fan 2100. Retrieved April 14, 2019 from museumofflight.org/aircraft/lear-fan-2100

The PPCo technique was developed by Diane Foucar-Szocki, Bill Shepard and Roger Firestien in 1982. Vehar, J. Miller, B. Firestien, R. (1999). *Creativity Unbound: An introduction to Creative Problem-Solving.* Williamsville, NY. Innovation Systems Group.

Firestien R. (2017, February 15). *Making the right mistakes,* Pamela Szalay with Roger Firestien and Cher Ravenell. Innovation Espresso [Blog post]. Retrieved from rogerfirestien.com/making-right-mistakes/

**Chapter Six – Plan for Action**

Rogers, E. M. (1995). *Diffusion of innovations.* (4th ed.). New York, NY: Free Press

Lessons Learned from 40 years in the creativity business. Kumiega, K. personal communication, January 15, 2019.

Roger image p135 courtesy of City of Fort Collins, CO.

CPSIA information can be obtained
at www.ICGtesting.com
Printed in the USA
LVHW071718180220
647330LV00013B/1108

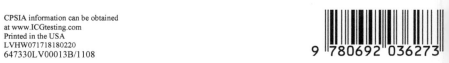